Karib

Karibu

WELCOME TO THE COOKING OF KENYA

Ann Gardner

First published in 1992 by
Kenway Publications Ltd.
P.O. Box 45314 - 00100
Nairobi - Kenya.

Kenway Publications, a subsidiary of
East African Educational Publishers Ltd.
Brick Court, Mpaka Road/Woodvale Grove
Westlands, Nairobi.
Email: eaep@africaonline.co.ke
Website: www.eastafricanpublishers.com

First published 1993
© Ann Gardner
Illustrations © 1992 Nobu Hirose
Reprinted 2005

ISBN 9966-46-987-7

Typesetting and layout by
Africa Global Perspectives

Printed in Kenya by English Press Ltd.
Enterprise Road, P.O. Box 30127, Nairobi

To my three children,
Liese, Fritz and Kit,
with love.

Acknowledgements

I wish to gratefully thank all the cooks in Karibu who gave me such a happy welcome; Gill Rebelo for her editorial tact; Christine Kabuye of the National Museums of Kenya for graciously supplying me with the information I sought on Maasai herbs; and all my friends in Nakuru and Nairobi who helped me out, put me up, and took me in — especially my cousin, Court of Appeal Justice Harold Platt.

I also wish to express my gratitude to Mr Michael Ochieng Odhiambo, whose example of hardworking dedication to his profession inspired me to do the same.

To all, *asante sana*.

Contents

Welcome to the Cooking of Kenya

"*H odi*," in Swahili, the national language of Kenya, means, "May I come in?" And the reply is, "*Karibu*" — "Yes, you are welcome."

Welcome into the kitchens of Kenya's up-country farmers, European highland settlers, Mombasa Arab and African traders, fishermen, housewives, city business people, and Indian merchants living in Kenya's small village *shamba*s and bustling towns, on her limitless plains and palm-studded beaches. Contemporary Kenyan history is written through their lives and in their cooking.

Although basic Kenyan cooking is simple, the people who live and cook here are varied; although cooking ingredients may be limited, each cook in *Karibu* turns these ingredients into dishes with a dazzling array of new and different flavours, firmly establishing a fresh cuisine to inspire and challenge the most jaded cook.

The cooks represented in *Karibu* have led the way in discovering the ease with which traditional tastes can be linked to new cooking concepts, creating exciting dishes. For example, Razia Khan has matched the fundamental staple spinach with a spicy yoghurt sauce to make a unique chicken dish; Peter Kimanzi has fine-tuned garlic and spices for his own Lobster Thermidor; on safari, Philippa Corse roasts her Christmas turkey in a pit barbecue; Emmanuel Mbema prepares fish in a delicate marinade of ginger, garlic, and lime, baking it in a coast-inspired fresh coconut sauce, but serving it with an up-country banana dish; Kihara Njoroge puts grated carrots together with green peppers and mushrooms in his Chicken

Nyandarua; P.S.S Darbar substitutes carraway seeds for traditional cumin in his Special Fish dish for a brand new taste; Marie Nasenyana prepares a delicate fish curry; Waheeda Khan makes a garlic chili paste that has a hundred uses. These are but a few of the cooks in *Karibu* who have created an extraordinary new cuisine, uniquely Kenyan—exotic, simple, healthy and inexpensive.

So we say to you, *"Karibu."* Welcome to the discovery of Kenyan cooking.

Market Day

*E*very day, all day, everywhere in Kenya it is market day. It is market day in the small village squares where produce is displayed on brilliantly patterned *kanga* cloths or on burlap bags spread on the ground; or piled two storeys high in the large, square, hangarlike concrete markets of Nairobi and Mombasa; or sold in small towns in open-air concrete-and-wood stall markets, from wagons along the streets, or from metal-and-wood kiosks festooned with bananas sold singly or by the treeful. Food in Kenya is a national pastime and everywhere for the picking.

Produce is frequently sold along the highways and byways. For instance, a traveller might load the back of his car with cabbages, onions, potatoes, carrots, and oranges when driving the Rift Valley road from Nakuru to Nairobi; or fill up on mangoes and pawpaws on the road from Nairobi to Nanyuki; or buy live chickens and fresh honey on the Mombasa-Nairobi road; or live rabbits on the escarpment road that winds along the edge of the Rift Valley. At dusk along the Kisumu-Nakuru railroad line, the train stops in places where there is little more than a few kiosks that glow softly with kerosene lamps. Women have been steaming elephant-size maize in the husk outside the kiosks. When the train pulls in, the women pile the maize onto metal trays and dart about hawking this delicacy to the train passengers who hang from the windows for the few breathless, hectic minutes before the train pulls out. After the train leaves, a litter of husks stretches along the tracks to mark its passing as the women pocket the coins that have clattered onto their trays and return to the kiosks to barter their profits.

3

While trading goes on informally everywhere in Kenya, cities and large regional villages have formal markets. These markets differ greatly in size and style between areas, tribes, and the size of the town or market. Perhaps the greatest contrast is apparent in the bustle of Loitokitok's market when compared with the sedate organization of the market in Lodwar.

Loitokitok is a hilly border town in the southwest of Kenya clinging to the steep slopes of Mount Kilimanjaro near the Tanzanian border. The treeless market square is lined with colourfully painted *hoteli* and small bright-blue, green, and red kiosks. When the brilliantly clad women of the town crowd together to buy and sell, the market is an almost perfect square of colour in an otherwise brown and dusty landscape. Being a border town, busy Loitokitok attracts people from a variety of tribes who have migrated there from all over Kenya. The informal *kanga*-clad highland women are joined by the dressy nomadic Maasai women from the plains below. Maasai women decorate and festoon themselves like Christmas trees, with beads circling their foreheads or wreathed around their necks or hanging from their ears like tinsel. They rarely have anything to sell, but come to the market to see and be seen, and to buy trading goods such as tea and cloth.

The Loitokitok market is noisy and bustling, with little organization. Sitting on the ground on clean, brown burlap sacks, women display brilliant piles of tomatoes and carrots; potatoes; *sukuma wiki*; small, hot green chili peppers; ginger roots; and large, plump purple eggplants in disordered confusion. One of the most popular vendors is a woman who sits at the edge of the market surrounded by mountains of pungent, sun-parched dried fish. The Nile perch and tilapia from Lake Victoria that she sells have been gutted, deboned, flattened, and spread out in layer upon fishy layer that resemble piles of thick, brown corrugated cardboard. Alongside the tilapia and Nile perch are thousands of tiny, iridescent dried finger fish known as *omena*. Drying fish is a necessity for the Loitokitok market because there is no refrigeration on the slow-to-go *matatu* in which the fish would have made the journey from the distant lake.

The market square in Loitokitok, its colours seemingly pasted onto the brown, hilly landscape, is in stark contrast to the Turkana market of Lodwar situated on the white, flat-hard desert lands of northwestern Kenya not far from the harsh, desolate landscape of Lake Turkana, an ancient, green volcanic lake filled to the brim with crocodiles and as majestic in its way as Mount Kilimanjaro. The town

4

of Lodwar itself is beautiful with doum palms intensely green against the white sand. This is the exclusive home of the Turkana tribe. The market is a sedate, almost graphic brown-on-brown. Because the very dark Turkana women dress entirely in brown goat skins relieved only by mounds of opaque dull-red, green, blue, yellow and black beads, the effect is as colourless as Loitokitok is colourful. Yet, to the Western eye, the Turkana market, cleverly organized and absolutely spotless, is one of the most exotic markets in Kenya.

The Turkana, a tall, quiet, graceful, thrifty people, make use of everything. There is no trash left lying around because there is no trash. The heart of the Lodwar market is an area reserved for the buying and selling of livestock and the domain of the men. Here, in the lacy shade of a spreading, pale-green umbrella tree, the nomadic men quietly discuss trade and news sitting on tiny wooden stools with leather handles that can be worn around their upper arms when they are on the move. The goats are gathered in their midst, and the trading is done with decorum.

In this Turkana market, a special area outside the market proper is designated for selling charcoal. Tall, square tin containers piled high with charcoal are neatly displayed in a line that forms an orderly circle. The women will buy the tins and carry them home on their heads like oversize stovepipe hats. And although the charcoal is precariously piled to overflowing in the tins, not a piece will be dropped or left behind.

Also sold in the market is a perfume called *apee*, the ground bark of a local tree which the women rub into their necks under their heavy necklaces of beads. The scent of *apee* is lovely: subtle and woodsy, but also mildly sweet. Down the road from the market, under the shade of trees where the women gather to visit and talk, the beautiful Turkana baskets for which the area is famous are made and sold.

Hoteli, or small cafés, are neatly lined up at yet another end of the market. These are spotless one-room mud-and-twig structures with a dirt floor and a fire in the centre for cooking and serving tea and *mandaazi*. When roofless, they are light and airy. Otherwise, they are quite dark, even at midmorning, with only the fire lighting up the customers sitting on low benches who have come for rest and refreshment.

The charm of the Turkana market, in this tree-shaded oasis situated in the desert sands of Lodwar, is matched by the kaleidoscopic array of tribes that throng the hilly border town of Loitokitok against the

majestic backdrop of Mount Kilimanjaro. But for the most eye-popping display of abundant, fresh, prize-winning–size vegetables and fruit, the Kisumu market stands out. Kisumu is a pretty town on a small rise along the eastern shore of Lake Victoria. It draws its produce from the lush western Kenyan highlands and from the lake region. With Lake Victoria spread out in the sparkling sunshine, Kisumu appears to be a miniature San Francisco. In the summer the weather here is exceedingly hot and humid, but in the Kenyan winter months it is mild, and the large market is overflowing with a delicious wealth of food.

Kisumu avocados are green or purple-black and the size of footballs. Here, the hefty pineapples are so sweet and nonfibrous, they are like candy. Purple onions are sold in sacks weighing 15 kilos (30-odd pounds), and garlic is sold in large bags of 5 kilos, an indication of taste preferences. Every imaginable variety of pumpkin and pepper is sold. Tree tomatoes and custard apples, along with mangoes, guavas, and every other kind of Kenyan fruit, are piled high in the stalls. And all types of grains and beans are stacked to the rafters in man-high sacks — or so it seems.

But Kisumu is not only known for its abundant food. It is also the trading centre for the blackened, ruffle-rimmed, pit-fired pots that are used for the storage of grain and water and are in demand all over Kenya, as are the heavy black-stone mortars that are crafted in the area. Both are popular trade items throughout the country as food and food-related items become a thriving business.

Down at the coast, the large concrete market in Mombasa is small for a major port and trading centre and has the feel of a bazaar rather than a market in the traditional Kenyan sense. The Arab-inspired foods sold at the Mombasa market are perhaps even more interesting to look at than to eat. Entirely square, the market is so packed with vendors that there is little space between stalls; nevertheless, it is sunny due to the open latticework windows, high along the two-storey roofline, which let in a ripple-patterned light. Still, the effect of the Mombasa market is claustrophobic and humid — a little like scubadiving among the ripe red, green, and yellow fruits and vegetables.

The largest market in the country by far is in Nairobi, the capital city of Kenya. There the Central Market sells fresh flowers cheek-by-jowl with fresh fruit, vegetables, beaded items, carved animals, metal bracelets, and baskets. Tourists love it. But most of the daily buying

and selling is carried on in two adjacent buildings, one for produce and one for meat, fish, chicken, and occasional live fowl such as duck. The produce market sells white radishes, Chinese cabbage, cucumbers, pencil-to-pin-thin string beans, and spinach along with the staple pineapples, bananas, pawpaws, tomatoes, onions, and green peppers. At the fishmonger's, the fish arrives fresh from Mombasa two times a week. Japanese housewives, in Kenya with their husbands on development missions, crowd the market alongside restaurant cooks, who snap up the extra-large prawns, parrotfish, sea perch, and squid.

One of the most unusual fish in Kenya is freshwater Nile perch. It is sweet, slightly oily, and tender without a fibrous texture; it is good steamed, marinated, sautéed, served in spicy sauces, and baked. Its flavour is so mild and its texture so tender that its versatility knows no bounds. Another popular freshwater fish is tilapia, often preferred because it is best roasted, fried, or served in stews.

The Nairobi Central Market butcher shop is full to overflowing with all cuts of pork, beef, mutton, and chicken, but the favourite meat among Kenyans is goat, which has less fat than mutton and is more flavourful than beef. Kenyans generally serve this meat roasted or boiled, and occasionally in curries and pilaus. Goats are kept in backyards in Nairobi and slaughtered there as well.

The *duka*s around Nairobi always keep fresh dill, watercress, and *dhania* (cilantro or fresh coriander). Most Nairobi gardens have plenty of parsley, fennel, and basil. Oregano is used dry, as is rosemary, although all these herbs are grown fresh throughout Kenya. I even found them growing in profusion in a cook's kitchen garden in sandy, dry Baragoi.

But be it a neighbourhood *duka* with a variety of fruits and vegetables; a small kiosk selling bananas, pawpaws, tomatoes, and onions; central markets bursting with all manner of produce, herbs, and spices; or simply roadside hawkers selling their fish, rabbits, and honey, Kenyans take pride in their produce from Mombasa to Turkana. And with good weather and fertile soil, the flow of delicious things to eat never ends. There are markets at bus-stops, at busy roundabouts, in shopping malls, and almost any place where people gather. Everywhere, all day, the market is open in Kenya.

Cooking Conversion Tables

S ince Kenyan cooks draw upon a variety of traditions, their cooking methods and ways of calculating temperatures and quantities often differ widely. The recipes are given as the individual cooks provided them, to preserve their authenticity. Should you wish to use another method, the charts below will assist you. If you encounter an unfamiliar ingredient, please check it in the Glossary (page 223.)

Oven Temperatures

°F	°C	Gas Mark	Temperature
250	130	1/2	Very cool
275	140	1	Very cool
300	150	2	Cool
325	160–170	3	Warm
350	180	4	Moderate
375	190	5	Fairly hot
400	200	6	Fairly hot
425	210–220	7	Hot
450	230	8	Very hot
475	240	9	Very hot

Weights and Volumes

	Imperial	Metric	American	1 Tablespoon
Sifted flour	4 oz	150 g	1 cup	1/2 oz
Butter or fat	8 oz	250 g	1 cup	1/2 oz
Granulated sugar	8 oz	250 g	1 cup	1/2 oz
Icing sugar	5 oz	150 g	1 cup	1/3 oz
Brown sugar (packed)	8 oz	250 g	1 cup	—
Grated cheese	4 oz	125 g	1 cup	—
Chocolate	1 oz	—	1 square	—
Liquid	1 fl oz	30 ml	1/8 cup	—

1

Asmahan Schmid

S unny Mombasa is reflected in the broad smile of Asmahan Schmid, a graceful Afro-Arab woman whose origins are in North Yemen and Eritrea. As a very young girl Asmahan lived in Tanzania at Arusha and later in the tiny Afro-Asian town of Arua in Northern Uganda. Her parents finally settled in Mombasa, where Asmahan was raised. Later, she was very well educated at the legendary Kenya High School in Nairobi. Begun by a determined woman from New Zealand, it was modelled after English schools so perfectly that pupils travelling to England for further studies often found themselves far ahead. Now the wife of a European restaurateur residing in the Nairobi suburb of Karen and working in the offices of Swissair, Asmahan lives her curious blend of Eastern hospitality and English manners with a quiet, well-groomed acceptance of everything life has to offer. Her broad and exacting education, together with firm Afro-Arab family traditions, have prepared Asmahan, a young woman from here, there, and everywhere, to walk all worlds in her past as well as in her present with aplomb, confidence, and gentle good humour.

Still, when the dust settles, Asmahan identifies herself more with Mombasa and the coastal people of Kenya than with anywhere or anyone else. Like Asmahan, Mombasa is a blend of the very old and the very new. While faded, ancient dhows in the old port are still loaded by men staggering up the gangplanks beneath impossible loads, English and American sub sweepers offload men onto Mombasa beaches for a little rest and recreation.

Established by Arab traders in the fifteenth century, Mombasa became dominated by the Portuguese at the end of the sixteenth century with the building of Fort Jesus, a formidable relic on the

13

island that guards the harbour entrance. The seventeenth century saw a bloody confrontation between the Arabs and the Portuguese with the fort as the focus of contention and power. With the disappearance of the Portuguese in the first quarter of the eighteenth century, the Arabs in Mombasa fought among themselves for the next one hundred years until, on 9 February 1824, the Sultan of Oman put himself and Mombasa under the protection of the British flag. It was then that Mombasa became the first British toehold in what was later to become the Kenya Colony and, with Independence in 1963, the modern Republic of Kenya. Although officially part of the British Protectorate of East Africa, Mombasa was still dominated by Arabs and Africans, and Asmahan's cooking reflects this coastal history — and also what happened next in Mombasa. In 1895 the English brought in Asians to build the Uganda Railway, and Asmahan's cooking characterizes Kenyan cooking to the fullest extent when she mixes Asian, Arab, African, and, with her marriage, European traditions.

When Asmahan married Rolf Schmid, he was already an established restaurateur. Trained in Switzerland, he has charmed Nairobi with his two restaurants, The Horseman in Karen and The Chevalier (eventually sold) in Muthaiga, both suburbs that were bastions of early English colonialism. If Rolf is a trained chef, Asmahan comes by cooking naturally. Since the age of nine, Asmahan has been busy in the kitchen. In Afro-Arab households, young girls are expected to start cooking at an early age. Relegated to chopping and cleaning up in her early years, by fifteen she was cooking entire meals for her family.

The kitchen was the family gathering place, so Asmahan spent most of her time there; as a result she is a very informal, social cook. That is, she might stop halfway through the preparations and inspect her rose garden or attend to her young children or tell me stories; or she might stop and have a cup of tea or show me her store, where she hangs her own meat for tender cuts and added flavour. She thinks nothing of whirring her whole spices to a powder in her electric coffee grinder — or of using the mortar and pestle for her garlic. The cooking goes on by fits and starts as she adopts any tradition that makes her life comfortable, seeing no reason not to blend together the best of all her worlds.

One of the best of her worlds is Rolf's nearby restaurant in Karen. Because cooking is the family business, Asmahan has too much of it

in her life to make it her life. So she often sends out to the restaurant for meals. A working mother, she is stretched to her limits and pulls every string she can to get little bits of leisure time. If sending out to the restaurant accomplishes this priority, she doesn't hesitate, and luckily she also doesn't hesitate to share Rolf's recipe for Chicken Kiev. But Asmahan is a beautiful cook when she decides to reinstate her own traditions — and when she has the leisure to grind the garlic, mash the cardamom, shred the coconut, and touch the Afro-Arab roots that are so dear to her.

One of Asmahan's favourite family recipes, using up-country staples and Asian spices, reflects Kenyan cooking at its best. This dish highlights the small-leafed, sweet, and tender vegetable *mchicha* that is so popular with Kenyans. Several bunches of *mchicha* are steamed, drained, and simmered gently with coconut milk, a bit of turmeric, cinnamon, cloves, a pinch ground red pepper, black pepper, and salt. Then Asmahan fries 1 onion, 2 to 4 tomatoes, and 1 green bell pepper until they are well blended and cooked down, forming a sauce that she cools and purées. Next she fries 3 or 4 cubed potatoes, drains them well, and sets them aside. She boils the meat separately in salted water until tender, then removes it from the stock with a slotted spoon. To the stock, she adds the purée and simmers until the stock is reduced, about 20 minutes. Then she returns the potatoes to the pot and adds the meat and *mchicha*. The result is a one-pot dish that Asmahan uses frequently. Typical of her cooking, this *mchicha* dish includes up-country staples, coastal coconut, sweet Arab spices, and hot Asian ones — a blend of Asmahan's past cooking traditions and wholly Kenyan.

Prawn Curry

2 medium onions, chopped
2 large tomatoes, peeled
1 small green bell pepper, cored, seeded, and quartered
1 green chili pepper, minced
8 garlic cloves, skinned
1 teaspoon vegetable oil (optional)
2 to 3 cups thick coconut milk
12 ounces prawns, shelled and cleaned
1 teaspoon ground red (cayenne) pepper, or to taste
1 teaspoon *garam masala* (page 220)
1/2 teaspoon ground coriander
1/4 teaspoon ground turmeric
Pinch salt

In a blender purée the onions, tomatoes, bell pepper, chile, and garlic. Add 1 1/2 cups coconut milk and simmer until the vegetable mixture is well cooked. Add the prawns, spices, and as much coconut milk as necessary for a thick but not dry sauce. Cook until the prawns are tender.

Or, if a blender is not available, mash the onions and garlic with a mortar and pestle and grate the tomatoes (see page 73). Parboil the bell pepper, then skin, seed, and mince. Mince the chili. In 1 teaspoon oil, fry the vegetables until the peppers are soft and well blended with the rest of the mixture. Then add 1 1/2 cups of the coconut milk, the prawns, and the spices, blending all well together. Add enough remaining coconut milk to cook the prawns and make a thick but not dry sauce. Serves 6

Spicy Cassava in Coconut Milk

1 cassava root
2 small onions, sliced
2 small tomatoes, skinned and chopped
2 green chili peppers, minced (see Note)
5 garlic cloves, crushed
1 teaspoon *garam masala* (page 220)
1/4 teaspoon ground turmeric
1/2 teaspoon ground coriander
1 1/2 cups thin coconut milk
Pinch salt
1/2 cup thick coconut milk

Skin the cassava and cut it into 2-inch-thick slices. Put the cassava in a pan with the sliced onions, tomatoes, chilies, garlic, and spices. Cover with thin coconut milk and bring to a boil. Add salt to taste. Simmer over moderate heat until well cooked. Add the thick coconut milk and cook for 10 to 15 minutes longer. The cassava should be tender but not soft. Serve as an accompaniment to a main course. Serves 4 to 6

Note: If you wish to make a milder sauce, remove the chili seeds before mincing.

Mombasa Curry

1 pound beef fillet, cubed
10 large garlic cloves, crushed
1 tablespoon salt
1 teaspoon freshly ground black peppercorns
2 medium onions, chopped
3 tablespoons vegetable oil or ghee
8 medium tomatoes, coarsely chopped
1 teaspoon crushed fresh ginger
3 cinnamon sticks or 1/2 teaspoon ground cinnamon
1 teaspoon cumin seed, crushed
10 whole cardamom pods, husked and crushed
1/2 teaspoon ground turmeric
1 cup cold water
3 tablespoons finely chopped fresh *dhania* Corriander

Rub the beef with garlic, salt, and pepper, and set aside for several hours at room temperature, or longer if refrigerated.

Brown the onions in the oil or ghee. Add the tomatoes and mash into the oil and onions until a sauce forms. Add the ginger and cook until the tomatoes are thick. Add the spices, meat, and cold water. Mix well. Cook until the meat changes colour, then cover and cook gently until the meat is tender. If the sauce is too thin, simmer uncovered another 15 to 20 minutes. At the last minute, add the *dhania* and cook for a few minutes longer.
Serves 4 to 6

Chicken Kiev

1 chicken breast, filleted, boned, and with a centre cut sliced
from the breast and set aside
1/2 cup all-purpose flour
10 garlic cloves, crushed
1/2 bunch very finely chopped fresh parsley
1/4 teaspoon ground black pepper
1/4 teaspoon salt
4 ounces unsalted butter, softened
1 large egg, beaten
1/2 cup fine bread crumbs
Vegetable oil

Lay the chicken breast flat on a wooden board, cover with plastic
wrap, and pound the breast flat with a mallet. Dredge lightly in
flour.

Mix well the garlic, parsley, pepper, salt, and butter. Roll this
mixture into a ball and wrap tightly with the reserved centre cut
from the chicken breast.

Place the chicken-wrapped butter mixture in the centre of the
flattened breast. Now wrap the breast securely around the butter,
tucking in the edges. Secure with wooden toothpicks if necessary.

Dip the breast again in the flour, then in the egg, then in the
bread crumbs, coating thoroughly at each step. Deep fry in oil
heated to 375°F. until deep golden brown, about 6 minutes. Drain
on paper, and remember to remove toothpicks. Place the crisp
chicken breast on a bed of finely mashed and sieved potatoes. Serve
with a side dish of freshly steamed garden vegetables. Serves 1

Sea Fish with Red Coconut Sauce

2 pounds sea fish fillets such as red mullet or red snapper
3 cups water
1/4 teaspoon salt
1 medium onion, chopped
4 small tomatoes, coarsely chopped
2 tablespoons vegetable oil
1/2 teaspoon *garam masala* (page 220)
1/4 teaspoon *dhania jira* (half ground cumin and
half ground coriander)
1 small red chili pepper, seeded and finely chopped
Juice of 1 small orange or 1 lime
2 cups thick coconut milk
Fresh *dhania* sprigs

Cover the fish fillets with the water and add the salt. Bring to a boil, then turn down the heat and simmer 5 minutes. Remove the fish from the stock and set aside, cover, and keep warm. Reserve the stock.

Fry the onions and tomatoes in the oil until thick, about 3 to 5 minutes. Add the spices and the orange or lime juice. Simmer for 2 to 3 minutes. Add 1/4 cup of the reserved fish stock and the coconut milk and simmer for 10 minutes. Add enough of the remaining stock to make a sauce of creamy consistency and simmer for a few more minutes.

Remove the fish to a serving platter and pour the sauce over all. Decorate the platter with sprigs of *dhania*. Serve with steamed green beans and leeks. Serves 4

Roasted Green Chilies

1 cup vegetable oil
1/2 pound whole green chili peppers (see Note)
2 tablespoons ground turmeric
1 teaspoon *garam masala* (page 220)
1 tablespoon ground coriander
1 teaspoon ground cumin
1 tablespoon salt

Heat the oil in a small saucepan to just below the boiling point.
Add all the spices and heat for a moment, then drop in the chilies.
Fry for about 15 minutes, or until the chilies are a bit blackened.
Remove with a slotted spoon and drain. Serve as a condiment for
curry. Makes about 2 cups

Note: If you want a milder taste, before frying split the chilies just enough
to remove the seeds.

Mombasa Coffee

3 cardamom pods, unhusked
2 cinnamon sticks
4 cloves
2 cups water
5 teaspoons freshly ground coffee

Boil the spices in the water for 10 minutes. Add the coffee and boil
5 minutes longer. Pour into a serving pot, but do not strain spices.
Allow to stand until the grounds settle, then pour into small cups.
Serves 4

2
Father Aldo Vettori

I t's nearly dark in Samburu District, and we've been driving all day from desert to desert: through brown scrub desert, white sand desert, pale-lavender and-ice-green desert, and trackless yellow desert. Piles of rock, mountain high, shade us for a stretch, the red dirt tracks us through a pass, then we slide more than drive down 500 feet on a narrow river of loose rock. The sun beats down as a barefoot Samburu boy races down the rocks after us, clutching a newborn white goat under his arm. Not many pass this way.

The development worker I am with is just as tough as the land and the people who have spent centuries wandering it. After earning his Ph.D. in zoology at Cambridge twenty years ago, Chris Field came to Uganda and then to Kenya, and the memories of the old university and a half-forgotten Europe still hang on him like his well-worn sweater. A consummate researcher, he has spent his best years in the desert country introducing the versatile, eco-friendly camel to the Samburu herdsmen, who, although still sceptical, are slowly replacing their well-loved though ecologically wasteful sheep, goats, and cattle with the newfangled humpbacks.

But today Chris worries about more mundane things. He worries about the inadequacy of his eight-ply tyres. Since twelve-ply tyres are hard to find in Kenya, we must stop and change tyres often, the victims of nasty, nail-like thorns that drop from the deceptively beautiful desert acacia tree, wasting precious time. With patched tyres Chris races over the barely visible tracks at a good clip of about 80 kilometres an hour to make up for lost time in our race with the sun as night closes in.

Chris has found what he is looking for just as the sun is sinking. We leave the desert and drive up to a small, flat, isolated, and lonely hilltop. The only landmark, hardly discernable on top of the hill in the gathering darkness, is a small chapel's steeple. In an otherwise empty landscape, the small cross on the steeple means a place to stay and a warm meal. It means four walls of security after travelling a sea of sky and plains.

As we drive past the small chapel and pull up to a half-finished — or half-begun — wood-and-concrete house, Father Aldo Vettori bustles out to greet us, grinning broadly with a suntanned, prematurely lined face toughened by years in the equatorial sun. Without a phone, he has had no idea of our impending arrival. Yet there is no hint of hesitation on his face as he coaxes us into his small house.

The bathroom, ambitious with a bidet, is nonfunctional at the moment, as there is no water in the taps. So we wash in pails of bright-red plastic, the precious water being trucked up daily in *debe* cans piled into the back of Father Aldo's white pickup truck. The rains have not started yet, but Father Aldo is energetically optimistic that his concrete catchment basin outside will be completed before they begin and will supply him with year-round piped water.

One room that *is* finished and well appointed is the kitchen, which is completely up to date and sports the latest Italian hardware. Father Aldo even has a refrigerator with a freezer. The stove is pristine white with trendy wine-red handles, and he serves us on his new country pine table complete with bone-white dishes and graphically modern red-handled utensils. He is justifiably proud of his kitchen. Although lit by a single bare bulb against the stark, whitewashed walls, it is quite fashionable.

More to the point, the new wooden table is overflowing with food. In happy broken English, often peppered with Italian and more often peppered with Swahili, Father Aldo prompts us to sit down to a full-blown meal of rich pasta soup, cold meats, cheeses, and bread. There is plenty of fresh fruit: mangoes, bananas, and pineapple. How he does it here in nowhere is close to a miracle. But it all seems so ordinary to Father Aldo that we relax and enjoy the bounty spread before us.

The dinner dishes are washed, dried, and put away as we talk about goats, camels, water, and food. Then Father Aldo begins to eye the possibilities of a kitchen-cum-bedroom; only Father Aldo's

bedroom is nearly finished. But instead we roll out our sleeping bags in the lean-to that eventually will be the entry veranda, intent on enjoying the fine, fresh desert night air. Father Aldo is stunned that we don't sleep in the small kitchen. It's warm and protected, he protests, and we can fix ourselves tea and it's close to the plastic pails. All very convenient, says Father Aldo, who in addition to being a fine host is also a very good salesman. But tonight he good-naturedly fails at this second calling and charitably doesn't say a word in the morning when we dig ourselves out from under an inch of fine silt that the wind has kicked up, howling all night long and blowing the dirt through the cracks in the wooden walls, the glassless windows, and the doorless doors. Compassionate and beaming, he has a full hot breakfast waiting for us. Then, following in the wake of his pickup truck, we set off to see the new reservoir he is building with the Samburu at the bottom of a natural spill area.

This is Samburu country, the home of a tribe that is among the most colourful peoples in Kenya. The *morani* of this nomadic tribe are some of the most beautiful men in the world, and it's hard to tear your eyes away from these carelessly confident warriors who wear only bright red *shuka* around their waists, their youthful bare chests and faces adorned with strings of beads, their plaited hair smeared with red ochre and adorned with more beads, hanging down their backs sporting sprigs of juniper, or caught up with lengths of flowered cloth. But Father Aldo's immediate flock are, more often than not, settled Samburu who have come to small towns such as Maralal to escape the harsh life of the bush, often finding the new life of the settlement even harder. Father Aldo's optimism is often all they have.

Father Aldo is in his fifties and has been founding small missions for more than twenty years, always in the farthest corners of the country. He is part of an Italian order of missionaries founded in the latter part of the nineteenth century by Padre Giuseppe Allamano from Torino, who, although he never put one foot in Kenya, had an uncanny feel for the needs and problems of the country. The order has settled mainly on the east side of Lake Turkana among the Samburu and the Rendille. Father Aldo is part of the Marsabit Diocese, which has its headquarters far away in Nanyuki, a small plains town at the base of craggy Mount Kenya. Of course, the rolling wheat-producing "plains" are deceiving. They rise to more than 9,000 feet in altitude and soon give way to Mount Kenya's foothills, which in turn rise to a peak of more than 17,000 feet. Father Aldo's small, lonely hilltop is light years away from the lush wheat fields and majesty of Mount Kenya. Here it is dusty — all goats, sheep, cattle, and the little maize that can be grown. But Father Aldo pays no attention to his limitations. He cheerfully flashes around in his small, white pickup, never sitting still, an Italian bundle of energy. There is just too much to do to consider the inadequacies of the desert. And today we are an added responsibility that he takes seriously, so he returns to his small mission in plenty of time to make us a lunch of goat liver and his special fruit salad.

Goat liver is the most astonishingly good dish. When my children misbehaved, I used to punish them by serving liver. Yet I couldn't get enough of Father Aldo's delicious goat liver. He has a whole freezerful and before he started on his morning's travels, he took out a portion of washed and thoroughly cleaned liver and sliced it into thin pieces. It is drying on a clean chopping board when we arrive for lunch.

Father Aldo has an incredibly light touch. With a twinkle in his eye bordering on the mischievous, he begins to warm a bit of olive oil in a steep-sided pan, slings sliced white onion rings into the same pan, and adds the meticulously cleaned liver to the whole mess. Then he gently stirs the pot with care until the liver is done. As if by magic, a lovely rich gravy of the oil and pan drippings collects in the bottom of the pan. He serves the liver with this natural sauce and passes a salad of freshly shredded cabbage, carrots, and sliced tomatoes. The whole meal is undertaken with great good humour and relish.

For dessert, Father Aldo proudly serves us one of his own concoctions, a fresh fruit dish that has the added surprise of avocados in a sweet syrup. This he follows with more cheese, bread, and espresso coffee strong enough to grow hair. The coffee in Kenya is unusually fine and is becoming a favourite of Kenyans, who are turning to coffee rather than tea for the midmorning break, although their rich, strong tea is favoured for breakfast and at five: a boiled, milky, sweet pick-me-up after a hard day.

Because of his isolation, Father Aldo could be forgiven for eating like a monk, but he has kept his generous Italian cooking traditions alive while imaginatively adapting them to fresh Kenyan staples, creating a softer, milder cuisine free of heavy Italian spices. The only imports he uses regularly are olive oil and pasta. Otherwise, he cheerfully enjoys everything that Kenya has to offer, from her coffee to her cheese and goats, which fall in quite nicely with his Italian customs. That's the beauty of Kenyan cooking: Its adaptability is always an improvement on old, tired meals, especially when accompanied by the gusto and appreciation of Father Aldo.

"Down the road," at another mission as remote as Father Aldo's, two Italian fathers are growing small orchards of apples, lemons, and avocados. But Father Aldo, newly established in Marijo, has not had time for gardens. His first priority is finishing the concrete water-catchment basin and the gutters for the house before the rains begin. Then his garden will come, as it always does in Kenya.

After lunch, Father Aldo is instantly in his pickup and heading down the small mountain to oversee the building of the reservoir. Today he stops to see that the trees higher up the hill have not been cut down for maize or that the goats and cattle have not denuded the hills so that when the rains come, the water will be channelled into the reservoir and not washed down eroded gullies. Reservoirs, water catchment, and the mission's small chapel are priorities in Marijo, as they are all over Kenya, and Father Aldo, a seasoned trail blazer, will give them his best shot, accompanied by his inimitable grin and hearty faith that it all will work out.

Goat Liver and Onions in Olive Oil

1/4 cup olive oil
1 white onion, sliced in rings
1 pound goat liver, sliced thin

In a steep-sided saucepan, warm the olive oil. Add the onions and sauté gently until translucent. Add the liver and simmer, stirring frequently. Serve the liver and onions with the sauce that has collected in the bottom of the pan. Serves 4

Sweet Fruit Salad with Avocados

1 cup water
4 tablespoons sugar
1/2 fresh pineapple, cubed
2 large bananas, sliced
1 firm ripe avocado, cubed

In a saucepan combine the water and sugar and bring to a boil. When the syrup is slightly thickened, set aside and cool. Add the fruit and avocado and refrigerate in a covered bowl or serve immediately. Serves 4

3

Christopher Murengu

*C*hristopher Murengu loves to cook. He learned at his father's knee when his father was chef at the New Stanley Hotel in Nairobi. While he was hardly old enough to see over the chopping board, Christopher helped his father to chop, slice, stir, and mince. That was fifteen years ago, and Christopher has never looked back. After apprenticing in and around Nairobi, he received training from an Asian chef and a Norwegian cook and has worked his way up through the ranks. As a consequence, Christopher can cook just about anything.

Now Christopher is beached in Lodwar on the white desert sands of northern Kenya, where he came to cook for the Lodwar Lodge and stayed on to cook for NORAD,* a Norwegian development group. Although he is far from the swish and dash of Nairobi, here he is his own man and fully in charge. He has taken over the menu planning, shopping, and cooking for the NORAD group and has it all his own way, to everyone's satisfaction. He cooks for visiting groups of development workers, teachers in seminar, government officials, and the occasional tourist. He may cook for one or for fifty, and on the limited staples available in Lodwar that's not easy. Yet Christopher's table is always overflowing with a variety of dishes, and no one is aware that he has planned everything down to the last ice cubes, which are as scarce as anything else in Lodwar.

Most of the fruits and vegetables, and particularly the *nyama* (meat), are brought in from Kitale, which is about three hours away. In addition, the NORAD development team often goes into Nairobi

---

* Due to diplomatic grievances, NORAD has ceased operating in Kenya.

3

Christopher Murray

and brings back the spices and herbs Christopher loves to experiment with, as well as dozens of loaves of bread from the famous bakery in Eldoret, which he keeps refrigerated, thanks to a generator set up by NORAD.

Christopher also has a pantry that anyone would envy. He has stacked cases of Cokes and Frescas, boxes of Kenya tea, and bags of Kenya coffee, as well as huge plastic containers of corn oil. The NORAD group is well supplied, and Christopher reckons that he has the best of all possible worlds: complete control over the menus and over an overflowing pantry.

Christopher has carved out his own legend, and visitors love to visit the NORAD compound and be diverted by Christopher's creative menus. He mixes Asian main dishes and Norwegian side dishes with impunity, and every now and then, he slips in his own tribal cooking. A Luhya, Christopher is especially proud of his traditional stew of meat, tomatoes, onions, and *sukuma wiki*, which is soaked up with *ugali*.

Ugali turns up all over Kenya, yet Christopher's is entirely different. This particular adaptation is well suited to European tastes, since his *ugali* has an unusually fine and soft texture; it's also less dry and has a great deal of flavour. To the usual 2 cups maize meal and 2 cups water, which are boiled together until stiff, Christopher adds 1 cup milk and a small pinch of salt. He mixes in 1/4 teaspoon butter just before removing the *ugali* from the pan.

For his stew, Christopher fries a finely chopped onion in 2 tablespoons oil and adds 2 bunches of finely chopped *sukuma wiki*. (You can substitute spinach or any green, leafy vegetable that is available.) Next he adds 1/2 pound cubed raw beef and browns it. The last ingredients are 2 skinned and chopped tomatoes and a pinch of white pepper. He simmers the stew for 15 minutes and serves it with hot *ugali* . (This stew is different from Emmanuel Mbema's [page 72] in that Christopher cooks the meat, *sukuma wiki*, tomatoes, and onions in a single pot. As usual, by manipulating staple ingredients, Kenyan cooks come up with two totally different dishes.)

We eat the stew and *ugali* with our fingers as is traditional. Both the NORAD bunch and Christopher love getting into the meal with their fingers. I simply can't picture eating stew and *ugali* with a knife and fork; it is amazing how the taste of metal ruins this dish. Even a spoon wouldn't do. *Ugali* is used as a *chapati* or bread would be: to soak up the gravy or sauce. It just takes a little getting used to, and Christopher prudently restores order before serving dessert by passing around a large, brightly coloured plastic bowl and a metal teapot full of warm water for washing our hands after the meal.

Although Christopher personally prefers home cooking, he is every inch the professional for the NORAD group. He's a kitchen guru and loves to talk cooking. For instance, he mourns the lack of avocados and *dhania*, favourites from his Nairobi days. You can almost see his eyes glaze over as he recalls the avocado-prawn salad he used to prepare, perfect as a starter, and he makes sure that I have the recipe for his own dressing. He also hates substituting parsley for *dhania* in his samosas and kebabs, but in Lodwar, what's to do? But Christopher is no complainer, and he energetically makes up for these shortcomings by pumping visitors for new recipes, which he tries almost immediately, adding his own touch by skilfully substituting available ingredients for those that are missing. He loves to catch us all out when he serves a new creation, and he sticks around to watch our reactions, getting a big kick out of our surprise. And we, catching on, give him all the fun back. Rarely have I found anyone so devoted to the game of cooking.

For instance, the fruit dessert that inevitably accompanies every dinner becomes the subject of our nightly entertainment. It is different every night, now decorated with little coloured sprinkles (where did he get them?), now mixed with custard (an English touch). Or some spice is tucked away in the fresh cream. Is it a pinch of cinnamon, or is it nutmeg? Christopher isn't telling, and he disappears into his kitchen as the debate deepens and we all but take bets. On a hot, sweltering November night in Lodwar there's little else to do, so we move our debate out to the veranda, where Christopher resurfaces — impish, twinkling, and beaming — to set up coffee, tea, sodas, and an occasional request for a late-night whisky under the brilliant canopy of stars. He's won the game, and happily retreats to clean up the kitchen as the night air grows thick with little bristling, darting bats. Sighing, we turn off the ineffectual bug lights as the debate finally winds down and the shortwave picks up the 9.00 news from Norway.

Mild Chicken Curry

Salt
Ground white pepper
1 teaspoon crushed garlic
1 3- to 4-pound chicken, skinned and cut into pieces
2 cups rice
6 cups water
1 medium onion, finely chopped
2 tablespoons vegetable oil
6 tomatoes, skinned and chopped
Pinch *garam masala* (page 220)
Pinch ground coriander
1/2 teaspoon ground black pepper
1/2 teaspoon ground nutmeg
1/2 teaspoon ground turmeric
1/2 teaspoon ground ginger
1/2 teaspoon ground red (cayenne) pepper
1/2 teaspoon roasted and ground *jira* (cumin; see Note)
4 garlic cloves, crushed

Rub salt, pepper, and garlic into the chicken pieces and roast in the oven at 350°F until golden brown.

Put the rice and water in a saucepan, bring to a boil, and cook for 15 minutes. Drain the rice, reserving 3 cups of the cooking water for the sauce. Keep the rice warm in the oven. Cook the onion in the oil over high heat until crisp. Remove the onions and mash them. Add the tomatoes, spices, and the reserved rice water. Cook until thick. Add the chicken pieces, garlic, and the mashed onions. Simmer all until heated through, about 15 minutes. Serve with the rice. Serves 4 to 6

Note: To roast whole *jira*, place seeds in a dry frying pan and stir over high heat until brown. When cool, grind with a mortar and pestle or in a food processor.

Samosa Filling

1 large onion, finely chopped
2 tablespoons vegetable oil
1 teaspoon crushed garlic
1 teaspoon crushed fresh ginger
1/2 teaspoon ground *jira* (cumin)
1/2 teaspoon *garam masala* (page 220)
1/2 teaspoon ground red (cayenne) pepper
Pinch ground cloves
Pinch dry mustard
1 tablespoon finely chopped *dhania*
Pinch salt
2 pounds minced beef

Fry the onions gently in the oil until translucent. Add all the other ingredients to the beef and mix well together. Fry with the onions until the meat is done. Drain thoroughly and cool before spooning into *Manda* or Samosa Pastry (recipe follows). Makes enough for 48 samosas

Manda (Samosa Pastry)

2 cups all-purpose white flour
1 cup water
Corn oil

Mix the flour and water together to form a stiff dough and divide into 12 balls of equal size. Knead the balls toward the centre and slightly flatten each to resemble holeless doughnuts and set aside.

Brush the tops of 9 of the "doughnuts" with corn oil. Stack 3 pieces of dough together, oil side up, and add 1 piece that has not been brushed with oil. Repeat to form 3 stacks. Now roll each

Continued

Manda (Samosa Pastry)

Continued

been brushed with oil. Repeat to form 3 stacks. Now roll each dough stack, using a rolling pin, into a round shape 8 inches in diameter.

Place one of the rounds on an unoiled griddle (Christopher uses a *sufuria* lid), and cook over low heat for about 5 minutes. Turn, peel apart each of the 4 layers of pastry, and remove to a cool work surface. Repeat with the remaining 2 rounds.

Cut each round piece of pastry into quarters as shown in Figure 1. Make a paste of a small amount of water and flour. Fold A to C and B to D as in figures 2 and 3. Paste along loose edges to seal the pocket. Repeat with the remaining pieces of pastry. Now open the pockets and fill with Samosa Filling (page 36). Fold the loose flap, E, over the meat and seal with paste.

Deep-fry the samosas in corn oil until golden. Serve hot with lemon or lime wedges. You may freeze any samosas that have not yet been fried for use at a later date. Makes 48

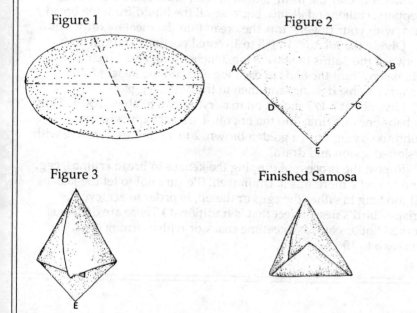

Figure 1

Figure 2

Figure 3

Finished Samosa

Kebabs

1 large egg yolk, beaten
1 tablespoon milk
8 slices white bread, crusts removed
1/2 pound minced beef or lamb
1 teaspoon crushed garlic
1 teaspoon finely chopped fresh ginger
1 medium red onion, finely chopped
Pinch salt
Pinch ground black pepper
1/2 teaspoon ground red (cayenne) pepper
3 green chili peppers, finely chopped
2 heaping tablespoons finely chopped fresh *dhania*
1 cup bread crumbs (optional)
3 large eggs, beaten
Vegetable oil

Mix the yolk and milk, soak the bread in it, and set aside.

Mix together the meat, garlic, ginger, onion, salt, black and red peppers, chilies and *dhania*. Squeeze all the liquid from the bread and, with your fingers, mix the bread into the meat mixture well.

Divide the mixture into 8 to 10 equal portions and roll each between the palms to make a log 3 inches long and 1 inch in diameter. Blunt the ends of each log and roll the kebabs in the bread crumbs, if using, and then in the beaten eggs.

Heat about 1 1/2 inches oil in a frying pan to about 350°F. Drop kebabs one at a time into the hot oil. Turn each quickly, and continue frying until a golden brown, 2 to 3 minutes. Remove with a slotted spoon and drain.

Repeat the process of dipping the kebabs in bread crumbs, egg, and hot oil 2 more times. Drain well. (Be sure not to let the kebabs sit too long in either the eggs or the oil, in order to achieve the crispy "bird's nest" effect that is traditional.) These are delicious served hot or cold, as a teatime snack or with morning eggs.
Makes 8 to 10

Norwegian Cabbage with Caraway Seed

3 cups water
1 tablespoon unsalted butter
Pinch sugar
Pinch salt
1 medium cabbage, shredded
1 heaping tablespoon caraway seed
1 tablespoon wine vinegar

Put the water, butter, sugar, and salt in a large saucepan. Carefully layer the cabbage and caraway seeds over all. Cover and cook gently for 15 minutes. Add the wine vinegar over the top. Simmer very slowly 60 minutes longer, shaking the pan occasionally. Stir and drain before serving. Serves 4 to 6

Christopher's Vinaigrette Dressing

1/2 medium onion, finely chopped
1 tablespoon finely chopped fresh parsley
1 hard-boiled egg, chopped
1/4 cup finely chopped or grated carrots
2 teaspoons sugar
2 tablespoons vinegar
1 teaspoon hot water
Pinch salt
2 garlic cloves, crushed
2 tablespoons corn oil

Mix all ingredients together and refrigerate. Serve with Avocado and Prawn Starter (recipe follows). Makes about 1 cup

Avocado and Prawn Starter

1/2 pound prawns or shrimp, shelled and cleaned
1 avocado, peeled and diced
Crisp lettuce leaves (optional)

Bring 2 quarts salted water to a boil and drop in the prawns,
reduce the heat, and simmer for a few minutes until pink. Cool the
prawns, and cut into pieces if large. Toss with the diced avocado.
Arrange in small cups or on a bed of crisp lettuce. Pass
Christopher's Vinaigrette (page 39) at the table. Serves 4

4

Elizabeth Ochieng

O n the tarmac road leading northwest from Lake Victoria to the small village of Bondo, which Elizabeth Ochieng calls home, we are suddenly engulfed in a yellow curtain of dust. A dust storm in Kenya begins with a wind that nearly sweeps people off the road. The only thing that holds the women down are the huge loads they carry on their heads, and their skirts whip about them as they vainly try to outrun the dust that slowly and inexorably advances down the road like an unexpected parade. The wind, mixed with the dust, brings a torrent of rain that pelts them as if all the washbasins of heaven had been emptied of their old, dirty water. As the dust storm marches up the road, a fresh, clear rain follows and rinses the countryside clean of dust. When the sun finally comes out, the land sparkles, and we get back on the road to Bondo.

Although Elizabeth went to school in Nairobi and currently lives in Nakuru, "home" is still in the Bondo area where she spent her childhood and where her parents still live. Home in Kenya can be anything from a few inaccessible acres shared by several wives to a 40-acre farm and compound housing cousins, nieces, nephews, brothers and their wives, and unmarried sisters. The latter characterizes Elizabeth's home. The family compound has two large, new, modern, concrete houses, a guesthouse, and other dwellings. It is a gathering place for the people of Bondo, since Elizabeth's mother is a leader in her church community and her brother is active in KANU, Kenya's ruling political party. So her home is a beehive of activity.

We arrive late in the afternoon, and because there are no phones, we are unexpected. A funeral is underway, and the compound is full.

41

Without a word, Elizabeth vanishes and immediately begins to help with the cooking. Her husband — by tradition treated as a guest — and I are immediately served with an unlimited array of sodas. He reads and I sit sedately in the sitting room with a few elders, sipping our drinks. As a good guest, I stay in the sitting room and am not allowed in the kitchen. Only when I evince a desire to see the cooking am I shown the kitchen.

The house is yet very new, and the kitchen is unadorned, a completely bare concrete room approximately 7 feet square. It has two *jiko* in one corner and a large, cone-shaped basket in another corner whose lid, when lifted, reveals a gaggle of somnolent chickens. There is another large cooking fire outside that will cook up an enormous *sufuria*ful of tea the next morning.

As night closes in and the cooking continues, we tour the compound by the light of a kerosene lantern and visit Elizabeth's grandmother, who is still living in a small, square, two-room, mud-and-twig house. In the entry room, the lantern is put on the floor and we are offered two seats. As women arrive from all over the compound, moving in and out of the lantern's spot of light, greeting Elizabeth, the whole effect is not unlike being in a theatre. Then, as if the curtains have just parted, her grandmother emerges, beaming, from her room wearing the new dress Elizabeth has brought her.

As the food preparation for the evening meal continues and a chicken is being neatly disjointed in one corner of the room, many come to take our hands in greeting, from the very old to the barely new. In the half light of the kerosene lantern and from the cooking fire in the next room, the brown dirt walls take on an elemental feeling of shelter that the two modern houses on the compound lack. Packed with happy, chattering, brightly *kanga*-clad women, the small dirt house is fundamentally safe and secure, perhaps if not factually, then at least spiritually.

Later, leaving Elizabeth's grandmother, we make our way back to the main house and pass perhaps thirty-five men who sit in a semicircle, silhouettes backlit by many lanterns, some dancing to a radio. These are the mourners. They will take turns dancing all night for the deceased, and even if the radio is modern, this tradition is etched in centuries of custom.

Under a night sky white with stars, in the deep quiet of Bondo, we are far away from Elizabeth's everyday world in the bustling railroad town of Nakuru, where she resides and works as a secretary to an accountant. Efficient and quiet, she handles her role as family cook like working women everywhere in the world — that is, her cooking has understandably taken on some standardization. But her culinary surprises are truly beautiful.

For instance, Elizabeth's *matoke* is the nicest I have had anywhere. Serve this instead of mashed potatoes and sit back and watch everyone trying to figure out just what you have done. It looks like mashed potatoes, but the taste is tangy and lemony, strong and impossible to identify, because this is a banana dish. Elizabeth mashes her bananas and puts no emphasis on a sauce, unlike Emmanuel Mbema, who uses a coastal technique (page 75). The result is absolutely wonderful with beef and other meats. The sweet *matoke* enhances the earthy flavour of meat, especially when Elizabeth serves it with roasted goat.

Roasted goat is one of my favourite Kenyan dishes, but if no goat meat is available use beef. Pieces of goat meat are simply brushed with a little oil and a pinch of salt and grilled until crispy. We pick them up with our fingers and suck out all the goodness, then crunch the crispy meat. This is not knife and fork food — but then neither are hamburgers, hot dogs, or barbecued ribs, favourite finger foods in the West.

Another creative use of a staple Kenyan ingredient is Elizabeth's *dhania* salad. *Dhania* is usually served sparingly and uncooked rarely, since *dhania* has a very strong, unusual flavour. But she experiments, serving the salad with a hot side dish of cabbage and as an accompaniment to her own brand of spaghetti. The earthy, tangy *dhania* salad makes these traditional dishes sparkle.

I stayed with Elizabeth in Nakuru for several weeks and was never aware of her cooking, although she always cooked the main course of the evening meal, *ugali* and *sukuma wiki* being prepared in advance by the *ayah*s. Elizabeth is so quiet that, although the preparations often took hours, I rarely saw or heard her in the kitchen. Yet she often cooks under extreme conditions, many times without running water or without gas. At these times she pulls out her small *jiko*, fills it with charcoal, and sits on a low table that also serves as a cutting board and preparation area to watch the pot boil — more as a relaxation after a hard day's work than as a cooking necessity.

A Luo with a traditional love for fish, Elizabeth's best dish is fresh tilapia served with a delicate tomato sauce that is truly fine. But her favourite is deep-fried tilapia. As a guest, I was offered the head of the fish, considered the sweetest meat. I gave up this delicacy to my host,

44

quite content not to eat what I could see looking back at me — but it seems that I was missing quite a treat. Still, old habits are hard to break, and Elizabeth and her family politely say nothing and are tolerant of my peculiar distaste for the finer things of life.

Elizabeth's day begins at seven o'clock in the morning and rarely ends until her busy husband returns home for dinner well after ten o'clock in the evening. By ten-thirty Elizabeth is ready to drop. The children have fallen asleep on the couches, and she picks them up, tucks them into their beds, and simply, wearily disappears.

Lake Fish in Tomato Sauce

1 tablespoon vegetable oil
1 medium onion, thinly sliced in rings
3 medium tomatoes, finely chopped
1 green pepper, finely chopped
Salt
Ground black pepper
1 2-pound whole tilapia, or other white fish, gutted
and deeply scored

Fry the onion in the oil with the tomatoes and green pepper until the sauce becomes thick. Add salt and pepper to taste.

In another large frying pan, slightly cover the fish with water and bring to a boil. Add the sauce, making sure to work it into the fish. Cover the pan and simmer for another 5 minutes, or until the fish is cooked through. Serves 2 to 4

Matoke

6 plantains or cooking bananas, peeled and cubed
1 medium tomato, cored and chopped
1/2 medium onion, chopped
1 tablespoon corn oil
Pinch ground white pepper
Pinch salt

Cover the bananas with water and cook until very soft. Drain and mash until smooth. Fry the tomatoes and onions in the oil, stirring often until they form a thick paste. Mix with the mashed bananas. Add pepper and salt to taste and stir over medium heat until warmed through. Serves 4

Dhania Salad

1 bunch _dhania_, washed, stems removed, and leaves
coarsely chopped
3 medium tomatoes, cored and chopped
1 medium onion, chopped
1 green or red bell pepper, chopped
1 teaspoon vinegar
2 tablespoons salad oil

Mix all together well and serve at room temperature. Serves 4

Kenyan Cabbage

2 medium tomatoes, chopped
1/2 medium onion, chopped
2 tablespoons corn oil
1 small white cabbage, chopped

Fry the tomatoes and onions in the oil until the onions are brown. Add the cabbage and stir over low heat until the cabbage is just soft. Serve accompanied by the *Dhania* Salad (page 46). Serves 4

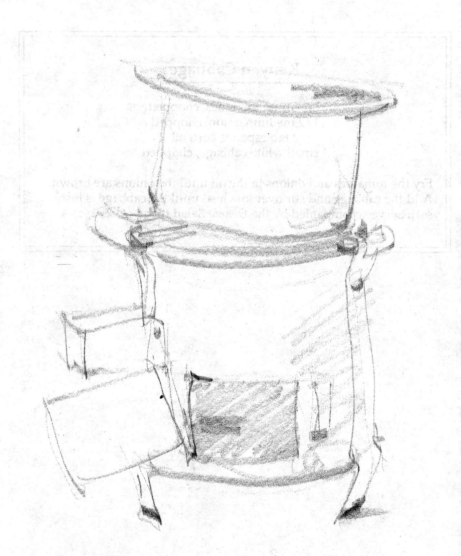

5

Hibaq Ahmed

ineteen-year-old Hibaq Ahmed, a Somali with roots deep in Kenyan history, is staggeringly beautiful, and although she keeps her mass of dark hair hidden under a plain headscarf and her body swallowed up in lengths of material, she turns heads simply moving from the kitchen to the restaurant of the *hoteli* owned by her mother, Mama Asha. Hibaq has been trained well by her mother and commands respect in spite of her youth as she runs the *hoteli* with aplomb, giving orders right and left in her low, tough-as-nails voice.

Hoteli is another word for restaurant, and Mama Asha's is perhaps the largest in Loitokitok. Set high off the steep, dusty street, which doubles as a river in the rainy season, it is in Mama Asha's *hoteli* that the villagers of Loitokitok start their morning with hot, sweetly spiced Somali tea and *mandaazi* flavoured with cardamom.

Loitokitok, a derivative Maasai name, is situated in the southwestern part of Kenya near the Tanzanian border, and from its perch on the slopes of Mount Kilimanjaro overlooks the Maasai plains of Tsavo. There are many people of many tribes residing in Loitokitok, and its nearness to the Tanzanian border makes it something of a boom town. Only its somewhat steep inaccessibility keeps it from booming out of control. Hibaq and her family have prospered along with the town.

Early one morning, Hibaq makes me feel absolutely comfortable and at home as we sit in the family's brightly decorated green-and-pink sitting room tucked behind the *hoteli*. She brings me sugary tea flavoured with cinnamon, ginger, cardamom, and cloves and discusses her family, of which she is immensely proud. Mama Asha herself has had no formal education and speaks no English, yet, left with six small children including a set of twins, has managed to educate her children and prepare them to take their places in Kenya as traders, a computer programmer, a diplomat's wife, and whatever else Kenya has to offer those who are determined. Hibaq is the third of Mama Asha's six children and the computer programmer; she studies in Nairobi when not running the *hoteli* in Loitokitok while Mama Asha is travelling.

Hibaq's eldest brother, Jamal, is busy planning a traditional Somali wedding. With her elder sister in Nairobi and the younger children in school, it will fall mainly on Hibaq and Mama Asha to feed and house scores of relatives that can number into the hundreds for the event. Some of the celebration will take place outside Loitokitok on Mama Asha's farm, where open fires can be used for roasting, boiling, and steaming the food. But throughout the days of celebration, most of the wedding dishes will be cooked on numerous *jiko* for which piles of charcoal will be made well in advance by Hibaq and the family. Today, however, lunch will be cooked on a single *jiko*, with everything measured to the last cardamom seed.

After we are finished with our morning tea in the sitting room, Hibaq leads me into the scrubbed-clean family kitchen, which is on the *hoteli* premises but separate from the restaurant's kitchen. As everywhere in Kenya, kitchens are the warmest, most hospitable places in the home, and Hibaq's is no exception. Kitchens usually are reserved for family and very close friends who help out, and it is not considered gracious for guests to sit anywhere other than in the sitting room. But today I am welcomed to watch the fireworks from a small, low stool as Hibaq fans the small fire in the *jiko* with her characteristic concentrated vigour.

Kenyan kitchens usually are informal places. These are not decorated showplaces with an armoury of steel and chrome and designer baskets full of unused cooking utensils. They are utilitarian and sensible. The elements of a Kenyan kitchen, especially outside Nairobi, where there might be no electricity, gas, or running water, are wood and charcoal smoke, boiling tea and sugar, spices, roasted meat, and a basket of sun-rich vegetables. More often than not the good smell of Kenyan soil and sunshine wafts through the windows as the breeze blows a fine silt into the warmed kitchens. And nearly every kitchen has its nearby herb and vegetable garden, adding the scent of freshly turned soil and green growing crops to the scrubbed

kitchens. The wooden table Hibaq uses for preparations, although new, is already velvet-smooth from the many scrubbings it gets. There is no smell of gas fumes clinging to dusty cooking utensils or the cacophony of blenders, food processors, and mixers. As a bonus, Hibaq, in her long dress, adds an elegant, exotic touch.

Hibaq brings Somali tradition to her cooking as she produces dishes that are entirely Kenyan but with a difference. That is, she uses the fresh if limited ingredients that she can get at her local market, and then adds her own mixture of traditional spices. To the abundant staples of rice, tomatoes, potatoes, peas, *sukuma wiki*, cabbage, pawpaws, lemons, carrots, garlic, purple onions, eggplants, and peppers, she adds, in various combinations, her favourite spices of cardamom, cloves, cinnamon, and cumin. The result is a different emphasis and different taste from any other cook's. I found this over and over in Kenya: Cooks using the same staples and spices, but with differing emphasis, created endless variety.

For instance, in a lightly spiced meat stew, the basic ingredients of tomatoes, purple onions, and meat that form the basis of up-country and coastal cooking is fundamentally changed by adding the staple peas, carrots, potatoes, and garlic and *then* adding cumin, cardamom, and *dhania*. I say *fundamentally* because Hibaq's combination of spices is not Asian or coastal but is an indication of her Somali roots, yet wholly Kenyan.

In a characteristic departure from Kenyan custom, she makes her stew by frying the purple onions and meat together in oil until brown, later adding the tomatoes, peas, and carrots, stir-frying until the tomatoes are saucy and the peas and carrots are still underdone. Next she adds 6 to 7 garlic cloves, 1 teaspoon ground cumin, and 4 to 5 ground cardamom seeds, and cooks them for another few minutes until all are well blended. Only at this point does she add water and 3 potatoes, peeled and cubed, and then simmer the mixture until the potatoes are done. *Dhania* is always chopped and added at the last moment before serving in order to preserve its distinctive flavour.

Although Hibaq cooks straight through from nine-thirty in the morning until two o'clock in the afternoon, and although she is also supervising the *hoteli*, she never loses her cool. She is not only beautiful and tough, but she is organized as well. She has measured out all the ingredients for the *mandaazi* in one tin plate and spices for the Party Pilau (page 56) on another so that I can see for myself just how much of each she will use. Since she has carefully planned and prepared the menu with only twenty-four hours notice, everything goes like clockwork. And even though she spends the better part of the day bending double over the tiny, hot *jiko*, her long dress and her kitchen are as spotless as they were before she began cooking. Her secret is her calm, unhurried attention to detail and an enviably strong back.

Hibaq starts the morning by cooking the *Mandaazi* with Cardamom (page 55), which is quite strenuous, as the large amount of heavy dough must be stirred, kneaded, rolled, and tossed around with a great deal of energy. Then, after the *mandaazi* are cooked and cooling, she adjusts the *jiko* and turns her attention to the pilau. Using a deep wooden mortar and pestle, she energetically mashes the garlic and cardamom together, making certain that the mortar and pestle used for the *mandaazi* and the tea is separate from the mortar and pestle used for garlic. This rice pilau must cook for at least half an hour. So in order to free up the *jiko*, Hibaq puts the pilau aside on the floor and covers the rice with wet newspaper, puts on the lid, then heaps the lid with charcoal ashes. The rice can now steam while she makes the Party Pilau Sauce (page 57).

At every stage of the preparations, she tells me a little about the dish, exactly what she will do next, and how she can alter the dish to suit different tastes and different occasions. In between these explanations, she talks about her dreams, her brother, the upcoming wedding, and the family. Then, finally depleting her histories and instruction, she turns on the radio, turns up Madonna, and, like the real teenager that she is, swings to the American beat. It forcibly reminds me that this capable, responsible, adult girl is only nineteen.

Turning down the radio, she seriously turns to the pilau's sauce. She is proud of her sauce and works carefully to make it the perfect consistency, as it will be spooned into the bowl with the rice, making the rice easier to eat with the fingers, so it has to be rich and thick. It is also the cook's signature, the product of her special use of ingredients that sets her cooking apart from any other's.

When everything is done to her exacting satisfaction, Hibaq serves lunch outside in the *hoteli*'s blue-and-white patio, exhibiting her sure sense of setting as an important ingredient of a successful meal. To underline her awareness of the importance of how a meal should be served, each dish is piled high with the rich, red tomato pilau and sauce as well as a bright orange carrot salad, followed by the pale pastel of her pawpaw and banana dessert — making the meal as pretty as it is delicious.

But Hibaq is not through. After lunch we retire again to the cool of the sitting room for more sweet tea and *mandaazi*. Then, much later, rested and satisfied, we sit around in the early evening on benches and chairs outside and drink more tea and watch the sun go down and the cattle returning home, silhouettes in the evening half-light against the deepening purple of Mount Kilimanjaro.

Somali Tea

2 cups water
2 teaspoons loose tea
1 unhusked cardamom pod
1 cinnamon stick
1 whole clove
1/4 teaspoon ground ginger
2 1/2 cups milk
Sugar

Bring the water, tea, and spices to a boil and simmer for a few minutes. Add the milk. Again, bring to a boil and simmer for a minute longer. Strain. Serve with sugar, or add 6 heaping teaspoons sugar before serving. Makes about 4 cups

Mandaazi with Cardamom

1 cup margarine
5 heaping tablespoons sugar
2 large eggs, beaten
1/2 cup milk
6 cardamom seeds, husked and ground
2 heaping teaspoons baking powder
4 1/2 cups all-purpose flour
1/2 cup water
6 cups vegetable oil

Cream together the margarine and sugar. Add the eggs and milk and mix. Add the cardamom and the baking powder. The mixture will resemble scrambled eggs. Add the flour and water. If the dough is sticky, add more flour. Knead well, working the dough toward the centre.

Cut the dough into 3 balls and roll out each to about 12 inches in diameter and 1/4 inch thick. Slice into 2-inch strips and cut these into squares.

Heat the oil in a deep pan. To test the temperature of the oil add one *mandaazi*. If it sinks, then floats to the top, the oil is ready. Do not crowd the *mandaazi* but turn them often until they are golden brown.

Remove to a plate with a slotted spoon to drain and cool. Do not refrigerate. *Mandaazi* will keep for a week at room temperature. Makes 3 to 4 dozen

Party Pilau

1 pound goat, mutton, or beef ribs, cut into 3-inch pieces
Salt
4 garlic cloves
9 cardamom pods, unhusked
2 tablespoons water
1 cup ghee or margarine
1 large onion, coarsely chopped
3 cups rice, cleaned
10 whole black peppercorns
8 whole cloves
8 cinnamon sticks
1/4 cup *jira* (cumin seed)
4 small tomatoes, thinly sliced
6 cups water

Boil the ribs in salted water until tender and set aside. This can be done the day before.

Crush the garlic and cardamom together with the 2 tablespoons water using a mortar and pestle. In the ghee or margarine, fry the onion until crunchy and brown. Add the rice, the boiled ribs, the garlic and cardamom mixture, and the peppercorns, cloves, cinnamon, and *jira*. Cook, covered, over medium heat, until all is nicely browned, about 10 to 15 minutes. Add the tomatoes. Cook and stir until the tomatoes are thoroughly cooked down to the consistency of a sauce.

Add the 6 cups water to the rice mixture, bring to a boil, and simmer gently, covered, until the water has been absorbed, about 15 to 20 minutes. Lift the lid and cover with a dampened piece of newspaper, brown paper, or linen cloth. Put the lid back on and steam in the oven at 325°F. for another 10 to 15 minutes. Serve with the Party Pilau Sauce (recipe follows). Serves 6

Note: The ribs will be used for the pilau, but trim 1 cup meat from the ribs and reserve, along with 1/2 cup broth, for the Party Pilau Sauce (recipe follows).

Party Pilau Sauce

2 medium onions, coarsely chopped
1/2 cup ghee or margarine
1 cup cooked goat, mutton, or beef (see Note, page 56)
1/2 cup, goat, mutton, or beef broth (see Note, page 56)
1/2 cup water
1/2 cup shelled peas
1 1/2 cups grated carrots
3 large tomatoes, coarsely chopped
1 cinnamon stick
2 tablespoons *jira* (cumin seed)
4 whole cloves
5 cardamom pods, husked
4 whole black peppercorns
5 garlic cloves, pressed
2 large potatoes, cubed
2 tablespoons finely chopped fresh *dhania*

Brown the onions in ghee or margarine until the onions are crispy. Add the meat and brown. To the meat and onion mixture, add the broth and the water. Stir. Add the peas and carrots, and simmer until the vegetables are cooked. Add the tomatoes and cook until the mixture forms a thick sauce. Grind the spices together with a mortar and pestle and add with the garlic and potatoes. Simmer for 10 to 15 minutes, adding 1/2 cup water if needed. Just before serving, add the *dhania*. Serve with Party Pilau (page 56). Serves 6

Kachumbari Salad

4 medium tomatoes, sliced
2 medium onions, finely chopped, washed with
salted water, and drained
3 carrots, grated
1/2 cup lime juice

Arrange the tomatoes on a plate with the onions on top. Place the grated carrots to one side. Squeeze the lime juice over all. Do not toss. Serve with pilau. Serves 6

Tangy Fruit Dessert

1 large pawpaw, peeled, seeded, and cubed
2 large bananas, sliced
Juice of 1 lime or 1/2 lemon

Toss the fruit together carefully. Pour the lime or lemon juice over the top and toss gently again. Spoon into small bowls. Serve with *mandaazi* (page 55) and sweet, spicy Somali Tea (page 54). Serves 6

6

Jackson Marefu

*T*he Kerio Valley, compact, flat, and boxed on three sides, is a valley within a valley. Situated within the Great Rift Valley, it is ringed on one side by the Tugen Mountains and on the other by the eastern escarpment of the Uasin Gishu plateau. It is the home of the Marakwet tribe. Somewhat isolated within the confines of the mountains, the Marakwet are a gentle, industrious people. Jackson Marefu resides in Arror, a small village nestled against the 1,200-foot escarpment, down which a magnificent waterfall, the source of the Arror River, cascades over a mass of bare rock from the plateau above. Arror is not 5 kilometres from the Benedictine Mission where Jackson has cooked for the last fifteen years.

Although Arror seems small to the uninitiated, it is a part of the larger community of the valley. For instance, schoolchildren of eight and ten years boarding 50 kilometres away from Arror think nothing of walking home for the holidays through the hot scrub desert of the valley floor, spending a night with friends, relations, or villagers along the way. The valley is closeknit for all its vastness and has created a sense of community among the hardy people who live in its dry, desolate, but scenic beauty.

Above the valley on the Uasin Gishu plateau, Eldoret, nearly four hours away, is the largest town and trading centre. It takes about half an hour to travel by car from Eldoret to Iten, a small town perched on the edge of the escarpment, then an hour down the escarpment in low gear on tarmac, and then three slow, hot hours for 52 kilometres along the bottom of the valley, skirting the escarpment on a dirt-and-rock road built years ago by the Italians. The only road leading from Arror to the escarpment road and beautifully executed, it is nevertheless fickle and changes character with the seasons. What is passable at one moment might be impassable the next. In the rainy season, the water flows off the escarpment above and floods the road with such force that it can carry a vehicle downstream — a stream that will be dry within a few hours, leaving the vehicle stranded halfway across the valley. And when the sun comes out, the road may have an uphill or downhill it didn't have before. But by the end of the dry season it is trampled back to normal.

Jackson himself is untouched by the problems of the tank-size four-wheel-drive all-terrain vehicles that manoeuvre along the bottom of the valley, bringing in roofing and fencing and other needed materials from Eldoret. He simply walks the 5 kilometres to and from the mission every day.

Jackson's home is perched partway up the escarpment, where it is cooler than on the parched valley floor. However, the family *shamba* is in the valley at the foot of the escarpment, where there is plenty of water for their millet, maize, beans, and cassava — crops that Jackson trades at a small centre 3 or 4 kilometres from the mission. Among the Kalenjin group of tribes, of which the Marakwet are a part, millet *ugali* is favoured over cornmeal *ugali* as the main staple of the diet. When millet is ground, it's a beautiful reddish-brown, almost purple colour, and when cooked as *ugali* it is very sticky — a little like eating peanut butter. Extremely high in protein, nourishing millet *uji*, or porridge, is popular throughout the country.

In addition to the crops they grow, Jackson's family gathers wild *chepkit*, a vegetable that grows over the valley floor. *Chepkit*, a plant barely recognizable as edible, grows closely over the ground, and is almost invisible to those who are not looking for it. Although it takes hours to gather, Jackson's family prefers it over European vegetables. Raw, it tastes a bit like mild parsley or turnip, or both, and has a nice earthy flavour.

Jackson is quick to smile, with a gentle twinkle in his eye. He is as proud of his six children as he is of his work, and he makes sure that I meet his son who is still in primary school — and to whom he looks for help in translating his language into English for me.

Cooking is a serious occupation for Jackson. He learned to cook at the age of seventeen after leaving his home in the Kerio Valley and making his way to Eldoret in search of work. He was hired by a South African as helper to a more experienced cook, and he later took over

as head cook for an English farmer. Jackson swears that he cooks the same dishes now that he cooked then, but in fact little remains of his early, European culinary education. Because of the nature of Jackson's job, which involves catering to often unexpected visitors, he is the master of leftovers and on-the-spot creations. "Waste not want not" is Jackson's philosophy. Whatever is left at lunch reappears at dinner completely transformed. He might have a run on a tomato base that appears and reappears as a sauce or a soup, a main dish or a starter. Or he might have a run on a curry gravy that he transforms into soups and stews.

For instance, if a bit of his curried mud fish is left over at dinner, it appears in the soup at lunch the next day. He simply fries a few chopped shallots from his kitchen garden in 1 tablespoon of oil, then adds 1 tablespoon of flour and mixes them well together. Next he adds about 1 cup of the leftover fish and its gravy, stirs, adds 3 to 4 cups of water to the rest of the pot, and simmers until it is ready, adding more water if guests have arrived. This soup is absolutely delicious with approximately 1/2 cup cooked rice added to the pot to make it a hearty meal all on its own.

Although Jackson's style might sound hit or miss, he has a unerring feel for what mixes well. He won't mix and match without a gentle touch and a sure feel for what is appropriate. If he has a leftover tomato sauce, he again starts with shallots and oil, adds the tomato sauce and cooked red beans, whole or mashed, covers it all with water, and creates another hearty soup. Once the cook is into the swing of it, leftovers become an easy challenge that is not only full of surprises, but easy on the pocketbook as well.

But Jackson is not only the king of leftovers. His curried mud fish is as spicy and hearty as his baked chicken is light and delicate, and he often executes a drastic change in the menu routine, perhaps serving light pancakes smothered in puréed pawpaws (papayas), lemon, sugar, and bananas as a light dinner. These dishes are European in concept, but Jackson has adapted them to suit Kenyan staples, Kenyan tastes, and the necessity of easy cooking for the least money on the slim choice of ingredients available in the Kerio Valley.

Jackson is a careful cook, meticulous and immaculate. Although his kitchen is large, the workspace is severely limited to a small counter that he washes down after each step in the preparations and keeps spotless. The spare cupboard above this countertop holds only ground maize, ground millet, sugar, flour and the spices cumin, caraway seeds, salt, and tinned curry powder. With these, along with what the mission can provide (the ubiquitous collection of cabbage, beans, tomatoes, onions, pawpaws, mangoes, and bananas, in addition to the sweetest and most finely textured grapefruit in Kenya), he prepares his variety of dishes. His own kitchen garden includes carrots, radishes, chives, shallots, watermelon, and cantaloupe. The mission also provides plenty of chickens, and local fishermen working the Arror River keep Jackson's kitchen supplied with fresh mud fish, a tender, mild fish that belies its unsavoury name.

Every morning Jackson makes fresh bread in heavy pans twice the usual size of a loaf of bread. In the mornings the mission people eat huge slabs of bread slathered with fresh butter and honey, along with the purple-red millet porridge, fresh cream, hot tea or coffee, and pawpaw, grapefruit, or bananas.

Rice cooking in Kenya approaches the category of a cult, and Jackson makes a nice, fluffy rice with his own version of the Kenyan ritual of pot watching. First, he simply washes the rice several times after removing obvious stones. Each time he washes it he carefully lets the water run out, carrying away any hard pieces he may have missed. After cooking the rice, he pours cold water over it, drains it, and lets it stand, then puts it in the oven to dry for a bit before serving.

But practically every Kenyan cook has his or her own special way of producing fluffy rice, and such secrets are guarded jealously. Some cooks wash rice by rubbing it repeatedly against the sides of the pot, some simply rinse it. Some let it stand in water; others insist that it should be washed first and then allowed to stand for an hour, drained. Some cooks cover the cooking pot with a cloth, newspaper, or dampened brown paper to steam the rice. Some, like Jackson, put it in the oven to dry. Others let the cooked rice drain over a pan and steam gently under a tea towel until serving time. There are those who insist that rice should be put into boiling water and still others who claim that it must be brought to a boil with the water. Many believe that a bit of oil is necessary. Some like their rice plain; others chop up onions and add spices to oil before adding the water and rice, making a pilau. These days rice is even grown in Kenya and is slowly replacing *posho* in some areas.

As for myself, I've of course found the foolproof method of cooking fluffy, dry rice every time. First remove any stones from 1 cup of rice. Then wash and rinse the rice several times until the water remains clear. Put the rice in a saucepan and cover generously with cold water, perhaps 2 cups water to 1 cup rice. Bring to the boil, and simmer on low heat for 10 minutes. Remove from the heat, drain off all the water, rinse the rice in hot water, drain again completely, and put the rice back into the saucepan to steam. Cover and let stand for at least 15 minutes. I cook my rice unsalted as it is usually served with spicy dishes.

Jackson shares cooking chores at the mission with another cook who at this time is on leave. But Jackson tracks him down and invites his friend and colleague to talk with me, eager that he be allowed to share his cooking expertise and secrets that Jackson obviously admires. Unfortunately for all of us, I have run out of time in the Kerio Valley and must leave, hitching a ride back up the escarpment with whomever is going, whenever they are going, however they are going, or it may be weeks before I get home. So I must forgo meeting and watching Jackson's colleague, which is a disappointment to all three of us. But neither man shows his disappointment, and I philosophically accept that I have missed a rare opportunity to spend more hours learning new approaches to cooking with limited ingredients — an art in Kenya, an art worth knowing.

These are lovely people, eager to share their lives with me. I have spent three days in Jackson's kitchen, warmed not only by his bubbling pots but by his kindly humour and infinite patience. Although Jackson speaks only the Marakwet language fluently, Swahili well, and English not at all, we have nevertheless enjoyed each other's company. His pride in his work and in his family, his unflappable ability to improvise when two are expected and twelve show up, his sense of security in a close community, his certainty, quick smile, and gentle fatherliness is a reflection of the people I met everywhere in the Kerio Valley.

Baked Chicken with Vegetables

1 3- to 4-pound chicken, cut into pieces
1 cup all-purpose flour
Salt
Ground black pepper
4 tablespoons vegetable oil
5 carrots, peeled
5 medium potatoes, peeled
3/4 cup coarsely chopped shallots
2 medium tomatoes, cored, peeled, and chopped

Dip the chicken pieces in flour seasoned with salt and pepper and fry briefly in the oil until golden brown on both sides. Remove the chicken and set aside, reserving the oil in the frying pan.

In another pan, cover the carrots and potatoes with salted water, bring to a boil and cook until just tender. Drain the vegetables, reheat the reserved oil, and add the carrots and potatoes. When browned, remove the vegetables with a slotted spoon and place in a baking dish, again reserving the oil. Arrange the chicken on top of the potatoes and carrots, and spoon a little oil over all. Cover and bake in a 375°F oven for 20 to 30 minutes, or until done.

In the remaining oil, fry the shallots and tomatoes.

For serving, place the chicken on a platter and arrange the carrots and potatoes around it. Pour the onion and tomato mixture over the chicken. Serves 4

Curried Fish with Chives

2 pounds mud fish, or other firm white fish
1 cup all-purpose flour
Salt
Ground black pepper
1/4 cup vegetable oil
1 tablespoon *garam masala* (page 220)
1/4 teaspoon ground cumin
1/2 teaspoon ground coriander
1/4 teaspoon ground turmeric
1 teaspoon all-purpose flour
1 tablespoon chopped fresh chives

Coat the fish with flour seasoned to taste with salt and pepper.

Heat the oil in a large frying pan and sprinkle the *garam masala*, cumin, coriander, and turmeric over it. Cook for a few moments, stirring frequently to blend the spices into the oil. Add the fish and fry for a few moments on each side. Remove the fish and set aside.

Sprinkle the 1 teaspoon flour in the spiced oil and enough water to make a thickened gravy. Bring to the boil, stirring. Return the fish to the pan, cover, and cook gently for a few minutes longer until the fish is done. Just before serving, sprinkle the chives over the fish. Serves 6

Jackson's Pancakes

4 large eggs, separated
Pinch salt
1 teaspoon sugar
1/3 cup milk
1/2 cup water
1 1/2 cups all-purpose flour
1 tablespoon butter, melted

Beat egg yolks well, then add salt, sugar, milk, and water. Add the flour and mix until the batter is smooth. Stir in the melted butter. Beat the egg whites until stiff but not dry and fold into the flour mixture.

Heat a lightly greased frying pan over medium heat. You can make these pancakes as thick or as thin as you like, just make sure to tilt the pan to ensure that the batter spreads evenly to the edges of the pan. Cook until golden brown on the bottom. Turn, and cook just until golden on the other side.

Top the finished, flat pancakes with Fresh Fruit Purée (recipe follows). If the pancakes are very thin, they can be rolled and topped with the purée. If serving for dessert, pass fresh cream at the table.

Fresh Fruit Purée

1 medium pawpaw (papaya), skinned and seeded
2 bananas
Juice of 2 lemons
5 tablespoons sugar, or to taste
Water (optional)

Purée all the fruit in a blender. Add the sugar and give it another whirl. Add water if you want a thinner sauce, and adjust sugar to taste. Makes about 2 cups

7

Emmanuel Mbema

Kalume Baya Mbema was born on the coast of Kenya in 1957. His Christian name is Emmanuel.

A slight, wiry-tough, fine-featured man, Emmanuel comes from the small coastal village of Kaimbeni near Kilifi. He belongs to the Giriama tribe, farmers mostly. The family farm is a small *shamba* that produces food for their own consumption. A very small herd of cattle and goats and a few chickens make up their wealth. Having very little money to spend, Emmanuel's family could afford to send him to school only up to Standard 3 (third grade). So at a relatively early age, Emmanuel left school to tend his grandparents cattle.

Although he speaks his native Giriama, he also quickly learned to speak fluent Swahili in school. So in 1972, barely fifteen, Emmanuel left home and headed for Mombasa, where he found a job and fit in well with a Swahili household. There he learned to cook Swahili dishes, a blend of African and Arab cooking unique to the Kenyan and Tanzanian coasts. Today, Emmanuel's ambition is to become a chef. He learns quickly, has a natural knack, carefully keeps his own recipe book, and is meticulous in the kitchen. As a matter of fact, he is a very meticulous man — neat in his appearance, in his thinking, in his planning, and in his attitude toward life. But turn him loose cutting, chopping, frying, and mixing, and he's a meticulous whirlwind: neat as a pin, but a nifty little tornado of energy.

Emmanuel attacks his coconut-shredding bench like a boxer his punching bag. He is never very far from the bench, which is fitted with a double-sided serrated blade, although the "serrated" edge is as coarse, sharp, and lethal as a swordfish's "spear." Made of very thick, heavy metal, each side of the blade becomes a shredding machine as Emmanuel rhythmically turns the coconut back and forth on the blade.

After shredding the coconut, Emmanuel pours water over the meat and mashes it between his fingers. He repeats this several times, extracting all the milk he can from the coconut. He reserves the thick first milk for his sauces. In the repeated "milkings" the liquid will become watered down, and he will use this thin milk for cooking rice. Later, he will throw away the coconut meat, since with repeated milking it becomes tasteless. If a shredding bench is not handy and a blender is, shell the coconut, pour out the water, remove the coconut meat from the shell and cut it into bite-size pieces. Fill the blender halfway with the coconut meat, cover with water, shred, and follow Emmanuel's squeezing and mashing procedure.

Emmanuel's basic staple is the coconut. He uses coconut milk in a green banana dish, in fish dishes, and in rice dishes; he even uses it to cook red beans that, when served over Coconut Rice (page 74) and accompanied by tiny, crisp string beans and red wine, is a surprisingly light but filling meal. Red beans and coconut: Only Emmanuel could have thought of it and made it magic. Sometimes he adds a tiny pinch of finely chopped *dhania* and, of course, a pinch of salt. He may even sneak in a hint of chili peppers. But basically, the best is always the simplest, and red beans drenched in thick coconut milk and served with Coconut Rice is one of the simplest and one of the best.

Emmanuel's Marinated Fish in Creamy Coconut Sauce also couples simplicity with maximum appeal. When he cooks this dish it is hard not to eat the fish before it ever gets into the sauce. You'll be tempted to just nibble, or serve it as an hors d'oeuvre in small bite-size chunks with pineapple and bananas, or as a starter with a little fresh lime. But *if* you can get the fish into the sauce without eating it all beforehand, it is a treat that your guests will not forget. In fact, hostesses in Nairobi have had Emmanuel come to their houses to prepare the dish for their dinner guests, and it's always a hit.

Emmanuel's favourite cooking staples and spices are coconut, cinnamon, cloves, ginger, garlic, ground red (cayenne) pepper, lemons, limes, oranges, bananas, tomatoes, and purple onions. He adds these to rice in pilaus, to fish dishes, and to vegetable dishes, changing the taste of the staple or meat with a maximum of flavour and a minimum of trouble. But Emmanuel's personal favourite is fried fish, the fast food of Mombasa. It is sold on the streets of Mombasa along with

fried cassava chips and thick, sweetly spiced coffee. The fish is simply spiced with salt, pepper, and garlic, then fried almost to a crisp. Another of Emmanuel's favourites is a sweet cooked at home in Kaimbeni village called *mkate wa maji*, which is like a very heavy crêpe made with a pinch of sugar.

Of course, Emmanuel also frequently serves *ugali* with a lovely meat stew. For one serving try heating a little oil in a small pan and sauté 2 tablespoons chopped onion, 2 tablespoons chopped bell pepper (capsicum), and 1 teaspoon finely chopped *dhania*. Cook over high heat until browned. Add 1 tomato, finely chopped; a pinch of salt; and 1/4 pound cooked cubed meat. Sauté for 3 to 5 minutes. Add 1 cup water and simmer until the mixture cooks down to a nice tomato sauce. Serve the stew with *ugali*, which is nothing more difficult than adding 2 cups maize or corn meal flour to 2 cups boiling water and cooking over high heat, stirring constantly, until the meal mixture thickens. Turn the *ugali* onto a plate, and as it cools a bit, form it into a "cake." Slice and serve with the stew and a vegetable dish. Emmanuel relies on *sukuma wiki* to accompany this stew. Heat 2 tablespoons oil and sauté 1 chopped onion and 2 chopped tomatoes. Add 1 bunch chopped *sukuma wiki* (or any other leafy vegetable such as chopped spinach or cabbage) and cook well, perhaps 15 minutes. Nothing could be better for you than this combination, especially if you have been eating rich foods.

Emmanuel's cooking techniques, as with most African cooks, are 180 degrees from Western techniques. For one thing, he cooks nearly all his dishes on a very high heat. Miraculously, he never burns anything. But he has had to learn to be quick. At home he cooks on a charcoal *jiko* that has little or no adjustable heat. With the *jiko*, it's as though everything is being cooked over a small fire pit. There's no subtlety to a fire pit, so Emmanuel has learned to vigorously mix his dishes to keep them from sticking or burning.

He also moves quickly when chopping garden-fresh vegetables such as *sukuma wiki* and herbs including parsley, *dhania*, and dill finer than a food processor or blender. In minutes he shreds meat off the bone with a knife duller than a butter knife. His fingers are asbestos: He lifts lids from pots that can hardly be touched ten minutes later. And he puts out flaming potholders with his bare hands. Watching Emmanuel cook is a spectator sport.

Emmanuel's cooking is a hands-on operation that he carries off with the skill — and the movements — of a matador. It's survival of the fittest in his kitchen. But if watching Emmanuel cook may be dangerous to your health, digging into his dishes is decidedly good for the soul.

Marinated Fish in Creamy Coconut Sauce

2 pounds white fish such as red snapper, red mullet,
parrot fish, or tilapia
6 garlic cloves, crushed
1 tablespoon crushed fresh ginger
Juice of 1 large lime
Pinch salt
Pinch ground black pepper
2 tablespoons vegetable oil
1/2 medium purple onion
1 medium tomato
2 1/2 to 3 cups thick coconut milk

Marinate the fish in the garlic, ginger, lime juice, salt, and pepper for at least 1 hour. Fry the fish lightly in the oil, then remove and set aside.

In a blender (see Note), purée the onion and tomato. Add 1/2 cup of the coconut milk and mix. Return the fish to a clean pan, add the tomato mixture, and simmer gently. Add more coconut milk to taste, but at least 2 cups. Simmer gently for 20 minutes. The sauce should be light, not thick. Serve with Coconut Rice (recipe follows). Serves 6

Note: If no blender is available, cut the tomato in half widthwise and grate it on the coarse side of a grater. Throw away the tomato skin. Slice the onions, then crush them with a mortar and pestle and mix with the tomatoes.

Coconut Rice

2 cups rice
Pinch salt
4 cups thin coconut milk, plus additional
2 tablespoons thick coconut milk

Put the rice, salt and 4 cups thin coconut milk in a pot. Bring to a boil, reduce heat, and simmer very gently until the rice is done, about 20 minutes. Watch the pot carefully and add more thin coconut milk if the rice becomes dry before it is done. Just before serving, add the thick coconut milk and stir. Serves 6

Easy Rice Pilau

1 medium onion, finely chopped
2 small garlic cloves, crushed
1 cinnamon stick, or 1/2 teaspoon ground cinnamon
1/2 teaspoon crushed fresh ginger, or 1/4 teaspoon ground ginger
Pinch salt
3 tablespoons corn oil
1 chicken bouillon cube
2 cups rice
4 1/2 cups water

Quickly sauté the onions, garlic, cinnamon, ginger, and salt in the oil over high heat. Add the chicken cube and mix. Add the rice and continue sautéing the mixture, mixing continually for a few more minutes. Add the water, bring to a boil, turn down the heat, and cook 10 minutes, uncovered. Remove from the heat, drain any excess water, cover the pot tightly, and steam 15 minutes longer off the heat. Do not remove cover. Serves 6

Green Bananas in Tomato Sauce

2 medium tomatoes
1 medium onion
2 tablespoons vegetable oil
1 tablespoon finely chopped *dhania*
Pinch dried oregano
1/2 teaspoon ground red (cayenne) pepper
6 plantains (cooking bananas) or underripe dessert bananas,
peeled and cubed
1 chicken bouillon cube
Pinch salt
2 cups water

Purée the tomatoes and onion in a blender, or see Note on page 73.
Heat the oil and fry the *dhania*, puréed tomatoes, and onion for a
few minutes over high heat. Add the oregano and red pepper and
cook together for a few minutes more. Add the bananas and cook
together over high heat until the sauce is well reduced. Add the
bouillon cube, salt, and 2 cups water. Cover and simmer on
medium heat until the bananas are tender but still firm, about 8 to
15 minutes, depending on the type of banana. Serves 4

8

Keiko Hirose

A collection of Kenyan cooks would not be complete without
stepping into the kitchen of a foreign development worker,
and I suppose there is no greater difference than that between
African and Japanese cuisine, yet Keiko Hirose has found that fresh
and abundant Kenyan produce can be adapted easily to her traditional
cooking. I met Keiko while we were taking a course in Swahili at the
Japanese Institute in Nairobi. She is in Kenya with her husband,
Nobu, who looks after the Japanese volunteers in Kenya and who is
also a dedicated, self-taught artist who spends his free time travelling
Kenya and painting the variety of people from the coast to the
deserts.

Soon after Keiko and Nobu were married, they became interested
in volunteer work in developing countries. To the amazement of
everyone but Nobu, Keiko took herself off, alone, to Ghana, where
she worked as a volunteer for two years. Then, after spending several
quiet years together in Japan, it was Nobu this time who went to
Liberia, writing to Keiko every day a detailed diary of his life and
daily challenges as a volunteer worker. He initially intended to write
512 letters to coincide with her birthday on May 12, but they soon
overflowed to 600. Keiko says that they learned as much about each
other during these periods of separation as they did together.
Characteristically, she philosophically emphasizes the best of each
situation, which is Keiko's charm and strength. She is adventurous
and inventive and ready to help smooth out and solve any problem.

Although quite essentially Japanese, Keiko nevertheless is her
own woman. That is to say, she excels in the traditional women's
occupations such as flower arranging, tea serving, husband pleasing,

and child raising, all of which she does with gentleness and a sensitive insight toward preserving harmony — but at the same time she promotes individuality in herself as well as within the family.

It is hard to adequately portray in words how Keiko recreates her ethnic environment in a foreign country in such a way that she bridges both worlds, showing her appreciation of each — a difficult accomplishment for the most dedicated and enlightened development worker and one that few attain. For instance, there is no better bargainer than Keiko, and when the vendors at the Nairobi Central Market see her coming, the good humour and respect is evident on both sides. The vendors always end up by piling her shopping basket with free pawpaws, a kilo of bell peppers, sweet string beans, or anything she wishes. But Keiko rarely takes advantage of such generosity and is likely to pick out only the long, white radishes that she grinds or shreds for her sauces.

Always concerned with health and well being, Keiko claims that white radishes are ideal for the digestion, and so serves them in a sauce with hard-to-digest meat dishes. For the white radish sauce, grate 1/4 cup radish and squeeze out the juice. Add the radish to 1 tablespoon soy sauce and 1 teaspoon lemon juice. Mix well. Serve in a small bowl and sprinkle on a little well-chopped parsley.

For an all-purpose sauce, mix 2 tablespoons sugar, 3 tablespoons soy sauce, 2 tablespoons vinegar, 1 teaspoon sesame oil, and a pinch of salt. Before serving, sprinkle in 1 teaspoon finely chopped shallots. Along with this sauce, pass the bowl of ground white radish. You can serve this with meat, rice, and stir-fried vegetables, but it's particularly nice with simple boiled meat, especially chicken.

I was amazed to learn that soy sauce is so essentially Kenyan. It did not, of course, originate in Kenya, but it is the product of a thriving industry in the country. Two Kenyan companies, Zesta and Cremex, produce soy sauce. It is on the shelf of every market in every major town and is used widely in restaurants. Only in very small villages is it unavailable, and then one can substitute diluted beef bouillon cubes, which is often handier.

Because Keiko serves so many dishes at each meal, it is not essential that her dishes be served piping hot. A stir-fried spinach and mushroom dish is cooked and set aside, along with an eggplant and string bean dish and a dish of snow peas and egg. The meat dish is often cooked last. But rice is always kept hot in an imported rice cooker, her one luxury.

Rice is served fluffy and steamed, boiled or fried, sticky and moulded, with sushi, or stuffed into squid. Keiko also makes a porridge of rice for tummy upsets. For this, add 1 cup cooked rice to 2 cups of hot fish stock flavoured with thinly sliced carrots and 1 beaten egg. Cook until the carrots are tender. The porridge will be a bit soupy but it is filling and easily digestible.

At nearly every dinner there is always some form of fish. A soup might be prepared with fish powder or fish stock. Fish is marinated, fried, served cold, hot, or raw, but it is always served delicately. She tells me that the Japanese don't care for the smell of fish, so she more often than not cooks her fish in a little ginger to mask the smell. Raw fish, especially in sushi, is often accompanied by a sauce of soy sauce, ginger, and horseradish. Fish steamed with shallots, soy sauce, and ginger is a favourite dish.

To get the pick of the freshest fish, Keiko is always up early on Tuesday and Saturday mornings to be at the fish market in Nairobi for the first load from Mombasa. She cooks kingfish, tuna, Nile perch, tilapia, and red snapper. But her favourite is prawns, the larger the better. She shows me how to pick out the freshest fish by searching under the gills. If they are a dull red in colour, they are fresh. But if it is brick red or brown under the gills, the fish is not fresh. Often there is a fine line, but if she is not absolutely sure it is fresh, Keiko will not buy.

The results of Japanese cooking are deceptively simple, yet difficult to execute. For instance, when I asked Keiko how to make tempura, thinking it contained flour and whatever else, Keiko said it was simply flour but that the art of getting the cooking oil just right takes some professional cooks three years to master. However, years of living in Ghana and now in Kenya has wedded practicality with art, and Keiko's cooking, if not precisely orthodox, is still a work of art.

For example, Keiko teaches me how to practically cook elegant sushi in such a way as to encourage even the most faint-hearted beginner. For "finger" sushi, form a portion of Sushi Rice (page 82) into a round ball. Pick up one piece of topping (cooked shrimp or squid, raw but very fresh fish, a piece of omelet, or sliced vegetables such as cucumber or avocado) and press it on top. For "barber pole" sushi, arrange finely sliced shrimp, cucumber, carrot, omelet, and avocado in slanted rows laid side by side on 4-inch-wide strips of cloth. Spread a layer of sushi rice 1/2 inch thick and 1 inch wide over the vegetables and press down lightly. Roll the sushi up tightly in the cloth. Then carefully turn the roll vegetable side up and cut into

1 1/4-inch pieces before serving. It is traditional to cover sushi with seaweed, but Keiko either leaves it unwrapped or wraps it in a paper-thin "pancake" of beaten egg (page 88) that has been fried like a very thin crêpe, turned out of the pan, and left to cool. This "pancake" or "omelet" is also used to decorate her finger sushi. Along with the sushi serve soy sauce and a little horseradish.

Another important aspect of Japanese cooking is presentation. Keiko loves to promote the art of visually enjoying food and decorates her dishes lavishly. That is, a simple platter of boiled chicken is dressed with rosettes formed by creatively slicing tomato skins. Little black sesame seeds decorate sticky rice balls. Vegetables subjected to delicate slicing techniques are used as decoration. For instance, cucumbers, celery, and mushrooms are sliced uniformly toothpick thin before they are used in salads or cooking; leftover meat is transformed when decorated with thinly sliced fresh green leeks; brightly coloured, thinly sliced carrots accompany a simple bowl of rice.

People say they never see Keiko cooking. That's because she's always in her kitchen, her natural habitat. Not surprisingly, drop-ins are common around lunch and dinnertime. But Keiko is never fazed. Despite the fact that she's knee-deep in children, helping Japanese volunteers with English and maths, and taking a course in African studies at the university, she always welcomes an opportunity to cook for you. This is Keiko's real talent: making you feel as if you are doing her a favour by sitting down to her dinner table.

Sushi Rice

2 cups rice
2 1/3 cups water
3 tablespoons rice vinegar, or 2 tablespoons cider vinegar
1/2 tablespoon salt
1 tablespoon sugar

Wash the rice thoroughly and rub the grains against the bottom of the pan in order to remove any husks. Drain and add fresh water and repeat until the water is clear. Drain and add water again and let stand for 30 minutes.

Now combine the rice and the 2 1/3 cups water and cover. Cook over medium heat until the water boils. Reduce the heat and cook 10 minutes longer. Turn off the heat and let stand, covered, for 10 minutes longer. *Do not remove cover.*

While the rice is cooking, combine the vinegar, salt, and sugar. Add the vinegar dressing and cut into the hot rice, mixing thoroughly. If you fan the rice with your hand while mixing, it will make the rice shiny. Cool the rice to room temperature. Makes 6 to 8 cups

Stir-Fried Prawns with Cucumber

10 large prawns
1 tablespoon sherry or white wine
1/2 teaspoon ground ginger, or 1 teaspoon ginger juice
1 cup vegetable oil
2 cucumbers
1 tablespoon vegetable oil
1 garlic clove, finely chopped
2 tablespoons soy sauce
2/3 teaspoon sugar

Shell the prawns, leaving the tails on. Devein and clean thoroughly. Marinate for 15 minutes in sherry and ginger or ginger juice. Deep-fry the marinated prawns in hot oil for 30 seconds until they become a bit brown. Remove with a slotted spoon.

Peel the cucumbers in irregular stripes and cut into pieces. Fry briefly and remove to a plate. Then, in the 1 tablespoon oil, fry the garlic and add the soy sauce and sugar. Add the cucumbers and shrimp and stir-fry a few minutes longer. Drain well. This is just one of Keiko's innumerable side dishes. Serve with barber pole sushi, *Yakiniku* (page 85), several simple stir-fried vegetable dishes, and an accompanying light broth. Serves 4 to 6

Satsumaage (Fish Cakes in Ginger and Dry Sherry)

1 pound fish fillets
3 tablespoons sugar
1 teaspoon salt
3 tablespoons flour
1 teaspoon ginger juice
2 tablespoons sake or dry sherry
Vegetable oil

Mince together all the ingredients except the oil. Make into small balls or any shape you like. Quickly deep-fry in oil over medium heat until golden brown. Remove with a slotted spoon to a platter, and serve with various dips: soy sauce and grated white radish, soy sauce and lime juice, mayonnaise and hot mustard, soy sauce and horseradish, tomato and chile sauce. Serves 4 to 6

Yakiniku (Thinly Sliced Beef and Pork in Marinade)

4 tablespoons soy sauce
1 tablespoon sake or dry sherry
2 tablespoons sugar
1 teaspoon crushed garlic
1 tablespoon sesame oil (optional)
3 tablespoons finely sliced leek
1 teaspoon grated fresh ginger
1 tablespoon sesame seed
1 pound tender beef fillet, sliced thin
1 pound pork, sliced thin
1 teaspoon vegetable oil

Mix the first 8 ingredients and use to marinate the meat for 15 minutes. Fry the meat briefly on each side in the oil over high heat. Serve with rice. Serves 6 to 8

Chinese Barbecue

2 pounds cubed chicken, fish, or tender cut of beef
1/2 tablespoon salt
1/2 tablespoon ground black pepper
5 garlic cloves, crushed
1/2 cup sugar
1/4 cup tomato ketchup, or 3 seeded and grated tomatoes
1/4 cup beef, vegetable, or chicken stock (optional)
1 tablespoon soy sauce
1 teaspoon salt
1 tablespoon vinegar
1/2 cup corn flour (corn starch)
2 large eggs, beaten
Vegetable oil

Marinate the meat in the salt, pepper, and garlic for 30 minutes.

Combine the sugar, ketchup, stock, soy sauce, salt, and vinegar to make a sauce.
   Combine the corn flour and the egg and dip the marinated chicken, fish, or meat pieces, coating them well. Deep-fry in oil until golden brown. Remove each piece to a bowl filled with the sauce. Marinate in the sauce for 10 to 15 minutes. If fish or chicken is used, drain and serve immediately.
   If cooking large pieces of beef, place in an oven heated to 325°F for 45 minutes to ensure that the beef is cooked and maximum flavour is absorbed from the sauce. Brush the meat with the sauce several times while cooking. Serves 6 to 8

Stuffed Squid Sushi

1/4 cup mushrooms, cleaned, stems removed, and sliced very thin
1 carrot, sliced very thin
1 tablespoon soy sauce
1 teaspoon sugar
1/2 cup water
2 cups Sushi Rice (page 82)
2 medium squid
2 tablespoons soy sauce
2 tablespoons sugar

Simmer the mushrooms and carrot in the soy sauce, sugar, and water until tender. Add to the rice to make a stuffing.

To prepare the squid, grasp the tail with your left hand and with your right grasp the tentacles at their base and pull. The tentacles and entrails will slip out of the body case. Carefully pull off the tail fins. Pull off the outer skin. Rinse the case and the inside well with water and dry.

Stuff the case seven-eighths full, as the squid will shrink when cooked. Place in a steamer and set over a pan of cold water. Bring water to a boil and steam for 5 minutes after the water boils. Cool and slice 1/2 inch thick.

Arrange the squid slices on a plate. Boil together the soy sauce and sugar until reduced by half. Pour over the sushi on the plate. Serves 4 to 6

Cold Noodle and Vegetable Medley

6 bundles Japanese noodles, or 1/2 package thin Italian spaghetti
5 large eggs
3 tablespoons sugar
Salt
3 tablespoons soy sauce
2 tablespoons vinegar
1 teaspoon sesame oil, or 1/2 teaspoon ground sesame seeds
roasted in 1 teaspoon corn oil
2 unpeeled cucumbers, sliced toothpick thin
2 bunches spinach, cooked, drained, chopped, and
cooled
2 cups finely sliced ham, boiled chicken, or pork

Cook the noodles in slightly salted water, drain, rinse well in very cold water, drain again and let stand at room temperature.

Beat the eggs with 1 tablespoon sugar and a pinch of salt. Pour 1/4 cup of the mixture at a time into a hot, lightly greased pan, swirling the pan so that the egg spreads evenly to the sides of the pan. Cook briefly and turn. Turn the resulting paper-thin pancake out of the pan to cool. Repeat. When all are cool, layer the egg pancakes and cut them into thin strips.

Make a sauce by mixing the rest of the sugar, soy sauce, vinegar, sesame oil or seeds, and a pinch of salt together.

Place the toppings of thinly sliced egg pancakes, vegetables and meat on a platter. Pass with a platter of noodles and a bowl of the sauce. Or arrange a plate for each guest with noodles followed by alternating spoonfuls of toppings around the noodles. Spoon over 2 or 3 tablespoons sauce. Serves 6

Note: You can use any raw, thinly sliced vegetable such as carrots; very thin cooked string beans; or thinly sliced cooked beets, well drained.

9
Khadjia Omar

K hadjia Omar is affectionately known as Zam Zam, or simply Zam for short. An Arabic-speaking Swahili born on the small island of Lamu and raised in the large seaport of Mombasa, Zam is a complex woman — yet one who leads a simple life centred around caring for her family.

Although she spent only her very early years there, Zam's Arab roots are in tiny Lamu, a picturesque and ordered Arab trading centre that has changed little over the centuries. By contrast, the old, sprawling centre of Mombasa, farther south along the coast, expanded when the British built the railway that originates in Mombasa and extends through the heartland of Kenya and to Uganda. Today, Mombasa is the main centre for goods distribution throughout the country. Bustling and modern, it retains little of the singsong aura of the early spice trade that still characterizes Lamu.

Zam's family originally farmed a *shamba* in Lamu and still owns five acres that produce coconuts, oranges, and mangoes. But her father, eager to provide for his growing family, moved them to the boom town of Mombasa, where he worked on the docks, eventually building three houses on a small compound for his married sons and daughters. But Zam moved on upcountry to Nakuru, where she married her husband, a financial controller for the Massey-Ferguson farm equipment dealership. Sheltered as a child, moved from the dreamy, isolated little island of Lamu to the complex port of Mombasa, and now living in the agriculturally oriented Rift Valley as the wife of an articulate, cosmopolitan, pipe-smoking man, Zam has, amazingly, kept her feet on the ground.

Since Zam speaks little English, her accommodating brother, Break, who is visiting Nakuru on vacation from Mombasa, lends a hand with the translating as well as with the cooking. We all start off the day with large cups of Zam's heavily ginger-spiced tea, which clears the sinuses, throat, and chest of anything living — a real wake-me-up. Then we all troop off to the Nakuru market, where Break fills me in on the merits of male bananas and the demerits of ill-chosen coconuts while Zam picks out five perfect specimens of the latter by shaking at least ten and listening to the amount of water in each. The less water, the better the coconut.

For the three main dishes, plus rice, she will cook today, Zam must shred five or six coconuts on her bench. Multiply this by 365 days of cooking, and one gets an idea of how many coconuts Zam will shred yearly and of how many hours she will spend sitting on her low bench specially fitted with a saw-edged knife for the shredding. Zam uses a handmade, cone-shaped woven basket called a *kifumbu* both as a receptacle as well as a strainer for the shredded coconut, neatly eliminating the several bowls Emmanuel Mbema uses. She simply fills the *kifumbu* with the freshly shredded coconut and adds a cup of water. Then she works the water through the coconut inside the *kifumbu*. The last step is to wring out the milk by wringing the *kifumbu*. The first milking produces the thick milk for the curry sauce. The second milking — adding more water and squeezing through the *kifumbu* again — is used for the rice and is much thinner. (For the blender method of preparing coconut milk, please refer to page 70.) With the rhythmic shredding and milking of the coconuts, the delicious smell and lazy beat of the coast begins to pervade the kitchen.

After shredding her coconuts, Zam turns to a heavy black-stone mortar and a baseball bat-size pestle to crush all her herbs and spices, bought whole so that the flavours remain true and fresh. When she works the coconut bench and then the mortar and pestle, the very rhythm and strength of Zam's patience settle the kitchen down, making the service and art of cooking a part of the family order with herself as the centre.

For her Chicken with Cardamom and Chiles (page 94), Zam begins by crushing whole peppercorns, and within minutes the kitchen is filled with the pungent trade-route smell of freshly ground pepper. She grinds, pounds, and mashes the peppercorns — not just a twist or two from her trendy clear-plastic grinder, but 3 full tablespoons of the hot black spice.

To the ground pepper she adds 2 full heads of garlic (or about 25 cloves) — garlic that has been peeled patiently by Break and his daughter. Now the scent of both garlic and pepper begins to prepare the senses for the pleasure to come, and everyone begins to anticipate the evening meal. Tummies are rumbling and mouths are watering. By now the kitchen is full of chatter, male and female, brother and sister, everyone enjoying the food preparations.

When the garlic and pepper are well blended, Zam adds 2 bunches of washed and carefully plucked *dhania* leaves. The resulting paste is a brilliant creation that rivals pesto for versatility as a base for pasta dishes, as well as for rubbing on meat for roasting, barbecueing, or stewing. Or fry chopped tomatoes in a bit of oil, add a pinch of salt and a pinch of the paste, simmer down, and spread on thickly sliced, toasted french bread as a starter. Add a dollop to stir-fried vegetables, particularly thinly sliced eggplant that has been placed in a pot with small slices of fish. Or add sour cream and salt to the paste and spoon it into baked potatoes. Add the paste to chicken bits simmered in yoghurt, then put the chicken in pastry cups; or add to a tomato-yoghurt sauce and pour over pasta. Add a bit of turmeric, cumin, and ginger for a curry. In a clean glass jar, the paste can be refrigerated and kept fresh for days.

Still preparing the garlic-chicken dish, Zam now pounds and pulverizes in her mortar the lovely combination of onions and cardamom seeds. This will be added to the paste later after the chicken has been boiled. The nicely pulverized onion and cardamom also make a versatile paste. Whip it into an omelet, for instance. Or make a batch of it, refrigerate, and sling it into your curries when you are too tired to start from scratch. The beauty of using the mortar and pestle begins to capture the imagination as Zam settles down to crushing the onions rather than using a blender or food processor. The slow mashing releases juices that are then blended with the crushed, perfumed cardamom, creating an undiluted essence.

After crushing the herbs and spices for the chicken dish, Zam turns to helping her brother and niece, who are enjoying the party in the kitchen. Together they finish skinning and seeding the bananas for a dish flavoured with coconut and cardamom. The banana dish is sweet and will be served with the chicken and the pungent Green Pea and Coconut Curry (page 95). The sweet, the spicy, and the hot are the essential combinations of the African, Arab, Portuguese, and Indian peoples who traded and cooked together for centuries on the Kenya coast.

92

In the late afternoon, Break and Zam are still cooking after a full day of nonstop preparation with only the early morning kick of the hot ginger tea to keep them going. Break is making a traditional fruit dessert with the absolutely essential ingredients of bananas, pineapples, and pawpaw. Passionfruit is often added for a more perfumed dessert. Although strawberries and watermelon are plentiful and particularly good in Kenya, they are rarely used in this way. Mangoes are eaten and savoured by themselves. This afternoon, Break adds his own touch to the dessert when he adds two bottles of orange Fanta soda and a little vanilla ice cream. He makes this dessert in the afternoon and refrigerates it for the evening, but as the sun goes down on Zam, she is still cooking, making a special custard only an hour before her guests arrive.

Zam makes her caramel custard so easily that I have to concentrate to remember that I am watching a cook. Although shopping, chopping, stirring, shredding, and mashing has taken all day, the meal seems to have come together without effort because it is all so essentially a part of Zam and her family's life. As she sits on the floor in front of the *jiko* once again, this time quietly watching the sugar caramelize, she is alone in her kitchen for the first time. One hour later, Zam welcomes her guests, freshly scrubbed, relaxed, smartly dressed, and with a smile on her face.

After dinner, upon request, she makes Mombasa tea. On the floor with her mortar and pestle for the last time today, she crushes to a fine powder a whole ginger root that she had dried earlier by setting it in the sun for several hours. Along with the ginger, she crushes three small sticks of cinnamon, several cloves, and several husked cardamom seeds. The pounding takes five or ten minutes. Then Zam adds the fine powder to a pan of water along with a very little loose tea — just enough for colour; about 1 teaspoon for 6 cups of tea — and boils all together for several minutes. The result is a very spicy tea. She does not boil the concoction with milk, as in Hibaq Ahmed's Somali Tea (page 54), but later passes milk and sugar for those who prefer them. Zam's combination makes an ideal after-dinner tea, since cinnamon and cardamom are natural snoozers, while ginger is a pick-me-up. There is just enough of everything to make everyone mellow.

While Zam has served her exotic dishes in a Western atmosphere of wine and pipe smoke, she has remained the soul of the enigmatic blending of peoples who have traded up and down Kenya's coast for centuries. Throughout the day, patiently pounding her herbs and spices, shredding coconuts, peeling and seeding a load of bananas, she has remained thoughtful and quiet, a woman with stories to tell: a woman who would, if she had the time, write novels.

Chicken with Cardamom and Chilies

2 3- to 4-pound chickens, cut into pieces
2 cups water
3 tablespoons whole black peppercorns
2 heads garlic, separated into cloves and peeled
2 bunches *dhania*, leaves plucked, washed, and finely chopped
2 medium onions
20 cardamom pods, husked
1/2 cup margarine
7 whole green chili peppers

In a large *sufuria* or soup pot, simmer the chicken in the water until tender, about 20 minutes.

Make a paste of the peppercorns, garlic, and *dhania* with a mortar and pestle. Set aside. Slice the onions, add the cardamom seeds, and grind together in the mortar and pestle. Gently fry the onions and cardamom in the margarine. Add the pepper-garlic-*dhania* paste and fry a little longer until well blended. Add the cooked chicken and its broth, and mix well with the spice mixture. Add the whole chilies and simmer, covered, until the broth has cooked down, about 15 to 20 minutes. Serves 16

Green Pea and Coconut Curry

2 medium onions, sliced
1 head garlic, cloves separated and peeled
4 medium tomatoes, finely chopped
1/4 cup margarine
1 tablespoon ground turmeric
4 cups thin coconut milk
Pinch salt
1 cup thick coconut milk
3 tablespoons all-purpose flour
3 to 4 green chili peppers, split
2 pounds shelled green peas

Pulverize the onion and garlic together with a mortar and pestle.
Fry the onion-garlic paste and the tomatoes in the margarine. Add
the turmeric, thin coconut milk, and salt and simmer together
gently 20 to 30 minutes. Whisk the flour into the thick coconut
milk, and add to the pot. Add the chilies and peas, and cook down
until the sauce is of the desired consistency. Serve with Coconut
Rice (page 74). Serves 16

Bananas in Coconut Sauce with Cardamom

17 large firm dessert bananas
1 cup sugar
10 to 20 cardamom pods, unhusked
4 cups thin coconut milk
2 teaspoons all-purpose flour
2 cups thick coconut milk

Peel the bananas, reserving the skins, then cut into thirds and slice the thirds lengthwise. (Zam uses male bananas, which are quite firm and need to be seeded. They also need to be cooked longer than ordinary bananas.)

Wash the banana skins and use them to line the bottom of a large sufuria. Layer the sliced bananas over the skins.

Whisk the sugar and cardamom into the thin coconut milk. Pour over the bananas and simmer for 30 minutes.

In a separate bowl, whisk the flour into the thick coconut milk and carefully add to the pot. Do not stir. Simmer approximately 10 minutes longer, or until the milk mixture is thick. Transfer the bananas without the skins to a serving bowl and spoon over any remaining sauce. Serves 16

10

Kihara Njoroge

*K*ihara Njoroge is a cook who obviously enjoys cooking. The
kitchen is his home, arena, and parlour, and he welcomes
me with a deep bow and offers me a chair. I am clearly
expected to share his day, which he is looking forward to with
enthusiasm. He is the spirit of *karibu*.

Kihara is fifty-seven and now cooks for an Asian family in Nyeri.
But he has been cooking since he was ten, when he started as a kitchen
helper in a European home. At that time, he had bravely travelled to
Nairobi alone from Gitathiini village in the lush, green Kenya
highlands, learning life from lonely experience. He was not to obtain
a formal education until he was thirty-two, when he ambitiously
enrolled in a night class for three years while cooking full blast during
the day.

A Kikuyu, Kihara prefers his tribal cooking to the Eurasian food he
has been cooking professionally all his life. Today he willingly cooks
Kikuyu *irio* dishes that he ordinarily never would cook, leaving this
to his wife, and does so with a great deal of pride and humour,
rubbing his hands together frequently with relish for the task ahead.

Irio, a Kikuyu word, is what is known in Swahili simply as *chakula*:
food. Of the numerous ways of preparing *irio*, Kihara chooses three
to demonstrate for me: *githeri, mataha,* and *njahi*. All three are absolutely
unique, even though they contain essentially the same ingredients
and are good examples of how Kenyans of all descriptions mix and
match a few staples to form entirely different dishes.

Although the *githeri* Kihara cooks for me today contains only red
beans, maize, and onions, one can add potatoes, carrots, spinach, and
tomatoes. *Mataha* is *githeri* to which he has added potatoes and

97

pumpkin leaves. *Njahi* is made with black beans and is served only at celebrations as the beans are rare and costly. The *njahi* is a dressy, pale purplish-pink and has the added touch and flavour of bananas.

Another popular *irio* dish is made with fresh green peas that have been soaked overnight, drained, and added to fresh, not dried, maize kernels and about 5 peeled and cubed potatoes. In a large pot, cover these vegetables with 5 or 6 cups of salted water and cook until tender. The amount of water will vary depending on the amounts of peas and maize. I couldn't pin Kihara down on these — just a couple of handfuls of each seemed to be enough in his estimation. It doesn't matter, he says, just use whatever you've got. Drain the vegetables, reserving the water, and mash everything together with enough of the vegetable water to make a dense "cake." Cool, and turn out onto a platter. This is called *cinjanju* and is very nice sliced and served cold the next day with a spot of spicy mustard. But generally *cinjanju* is a substitute for *ugali* and is similarly used to scoop up stews with the fingers.

Kihara explains that *posho ugali* is never served with *irio*, since one never serves maize with maize. To serve *posho* with *irio* would be like serving potatoes with pasta at the same meal. These aesthetics aside, the colours of *irio*, ranging from the pale green of *cinjanju* to the pale lavender of *njahi*, are truly beautiful. It's also hearty and filling, and the pocketbook is still heavy with shillings after returning from the market with a full basket.

Even though beans, maize, and bananas grow in the family *shamba*, Kihara's wife, also a resident of the bustling town of Nyeri, buys everything at the market. Kihara assures me that her garden is just for looking as it is too small to feed her family. He chuckles when he likens her vegetable and fruit garden to the Westerner's flower gardens: mostly for looking, just to make her feel good.

The market in the Central Highlands town of Nyeri, which is not far from the rainy-lush Aberdare Mountains, is reminiscent of a nineteenth-century European village market. The main building is a large, open-air, high-pitched, wooden-raftered shed with a dirt floor and wood-slatted stalls lined with burlap sacking. The food also is buried deep in brownish-gray burlap and is lost to view in the dusty gloom of the shed. As the weak, overcast highland sunshine rarely penetrates the interior of the market, the whole effect is quite dampening. But beyond the large wooden shed is a small courtyard alive with children and chickens chasing each other under a huge,

spreading tree. The happy noises in the gaily painted courtyard more than make up for the sobriety of the main market.

Energetic Kihara has already been to the market by the time I arrive at the home of the local builder for whom he works, and the kitchen is already steaming with tins of fresh tarts filled with honey and coconut that he has just pulled from the oven. Beans are soaking, and a chicken has been washed and thrown in the pot, looking very well plucked and scrubbed.

Kihara is fascinating to watch. He rarely uses a spoon, preferring to get his fingers right into the food as he tests the beans, pinching them as well as the potatoes to see if they are done. Moving quickly, he takes the corn off the cob with his fingers and peels the courgettes (zucchini) with his fingers as well — not a small feat, but one that he makes look simple. When he cooks the chicken dish, he mixes the vegetables in the frying pan with his fingertips. Consequently, he washes and dries his hands frequently. So Kihara is a busy cook, washing, drying, and rubbing his hands together in great delight as he plunges them again into the pots, testing, pinching, squeezing, mixing, and peeling.

After cooking three of his traditional dishes all at the same time, he begins his Chicken Nyandarua (page 103), which he has named after the nearby Aberdare Mountains in whose rain forests he worked as a chef at the popular game lodge The Ark. Kihara is full of surprises, and I wonder what else he has done in his full fifty-seven years.

Chicken Nyandarua, like *irio*, is the very spirit of Kenyan cooking. Although European in concept, it is essentially and fundamentally up-country Kenyan cooking in its simplicity and reliance on fresh flavours and delicate herbs and spices. Kihara tells me that Kikuyus traditionally don't cook with herbs, not even the ubiquitous *dhania*. And they are not great bird or fish eaters, preferring mutton and beef either stewed, boiled, or roasted. However, he will eat chicken, which the elders of his clan to this day will not touch. So Kihara, like other adventurous Kenyan cooks, is experimenting with sense and sensibility and devising a wholly satisfying new cuisine.

Chicken Nyandarua is a favourite with everyone and has never let me down. Served with a light broth starter, accompanied by parsleyed potatoes, and followed by puckery-sweet stewed fruit, the meal, free of heavy spices, is easy on the tummy and a wonderful balm after a hard day. This is the beauty of Kenya's up-country cooking, the hallmark of its popularity.

The simple, healthy staples of up-country cooking include ground millet, beans, maize, tomatoes, *sukuma wiki*, carrots, cabbage, onions, potatoes, bananas, and pawpaws. Simple, yes; easy on the heart, yes; and foods that soothe any number of stress-related diseases. I rarely mix up-country cooking with spicy coastal or hot Asian dishes. Although Kenyan cooking is a rich blend of all three regional and ethnic approaches, I'm always glad to get back to the basics of up-country cooking, and I am appreciative of Kihara's patient pride in teaching me about this particular aspect of Kenyan cuisine.

Now that his duties in the kitchen are finished and he can see that I am well satisfied, Kihara relaxes, takes off his apron, and sits down to a late afternoon chitchat as if has known me for a lifetime.

Githeri

1/2 pound dried red beans
1 pound dried maize
Salt
3 medium onions, chopped
1 tablespoon vegetable oil

Cover the red beans and maize with water and soak overnight. Drain. Cover again with water, add salt to taste, and boil gently for 2 1/2 hours, or until the beans and maize are soft. Drain and set aside. Fry the onions in the oil until soft. Add to the beans and maize before serving. Serves 4

Mataha

1/2 pound dried red beans
1 pound dried maize
Salt
8 medium potatoes, peeled and cubed
10 pumpkin leaves, coarsely chopped

Soak the beans and maize overnight in water to cover. Drain, cover
again with water, add salt to taste, and boil gently for 2 1/2 hours,
or until soft. Drain and set aside. Cover the potatoes with water
and boil until nearly soft. Add the pumpkin leaves and cook until
tender. Drain. Add to the maize and beans, and mash all together.
The mixture should be dense and firm. Adjust salt to taste.
Serves 4 to 6

Njahi

1 pound black beans
Salt
5 medium potatoes, peeled and chopped
5 plantains (cooking bananas) or underripe dessert bananas,
peeled and cut into small pieces.

Soak the black beans overnight in water to cover. Drain, cover
again with water, add salt to taste, and boil gently for 2 1/2 hours,
or until tender. Drain and set aside. Cover the potatoes and
bananas with water and boil until tender. Drain, then add to the
beans and mash all together. The mixture should be firm. Adjust
salt to taste. Serves 4

Chicken Nyandarua

1 2-pound chicken, cut into 8 pieces
All-purpose flour
Salt
Ground black pepper
2 tablespoons vegetable oil
3 medium onions, chopped
1 cup sliced fresh mushrooms
5 medium tomatoes, chopped
2 carrots, finely grated
2 whole cloves
1 bay leaf

Dust the chicken with flour seasoned with salt and pepper. Warm 1 tablespoon oil in a large frying pan over medium heat and brown the chicken pieces on both sides. Remove the chicken from the pan and drain.

In another pan, warm the remaining 1 tablespoon oil, add the vegetables and cloves, and stir-fry gently until the carrots are tender, about five minutes. The mixture will be thick. Put the chicken into a baking dish with the bay leaf and cover well with the vegetable mixture. Bake in the oven at 375° F. for 30 minutes, or until the chicken is done. Serves 4

11

Marie Nasenyana

*M*arie Nasenyana, a tall, proud, dignified Turkana woman, is an anomaly in these parts. Only twenty-one, she is the energetic leader of a twenty-member women's cooperative that runs a bakery, a store, a catering service, a waterworks, and a brickworks. To appreciate the miracle of these seemingly mundane activities, one has to see and appreciate Lodwar, the town in which Marie resides.

On the western side of Lake Turkana, the tarmac road north ends at Lodwar. Beyond Lodwar is camel country. Lodwar itself is all doum palm and white sand, lovely but hardly bustling. A few piles of rocks break the horizon, but Lodwar is basically set in flat, white desert interrupted only by the beautiful Turkwel River. Broad, palm-lined, muddy, and, in the rainy season, roaring, it is nevertheless a welcome landmark in an otherwise trackless landscape.

Although Marie no longer lives in the bush but in a settlement, her living arrangement is basically traditional. That is, she lives with her husband and two children in an *aui*. An *aui* is a circular-shaped compound entirely fenced in palm thatch and containing the husband's one-room palm-thatched *ekol* and each of his wives' *ekol*s. Outside each wife's *ekol* is a crescent-shaped, roofless thatched area, in the middle of which burns the cooking fire. Fed continuously with twigs and logs, the fire is nestled within the circle of three large stones that hold the cooking pot. In a settlement household, the cooking pot is kept bubbling with *posho*, beans and maize, or tea throughout the day, although in the bush none of these staples is traditional or necessarily desired. In both bush and settlement *aui*, fenced *boma*s shelter the livestock; a separate hut might also be used for the drying

105

of meat, the storage of milk in gourds, and as a shelter for young goats.

Physically ordered along the lines of known traditions, Marie's life has been made difficult by the profound change of settlement living. She has had to learn a new way of life, new customs, new ideas, and a whole new technology, as has her husband. Although the bush supports the nomads and their way of life, the men in settlements and villages who have been herdsmen often find themselves jobless, and it has fallen to the women to creatively make use of their cooking, building, farming, basketry, and sewing skills to bring in money to help support the family.

Marie at fifteen had her first child, and times were hard. With no skills and little education, she had little to offer her struggling husband by way of a means of earning money. But within a stone's throw of Marie's small settlement, a NORAD development group had set up housekeeping, and a Swedish doctor and his wife, Cissie, had joined the NORAD compound. Cissie, a red-haired, clear-eyed, energetic mother of two children and five adopted children of different nationalities, decided to start her own development project: a bakery. She put out the word, inviting the Turkana women from the village around her compound to come and learn to bake. Only Marie and two others showed up.

Undaunted by the lack of response, Cissie launched her project by teaching Marie how to bake bread and scones using the facilities of her own kitchen. But it soon became clear to Cissie that when she left the country and returned to Sweden, the women would be back to square one without her stove and running water. So she decided to teach them how to build their own brick oven, and this oven, still going strong, was the beginning of the Nawoitorong Women's Cooperative. Started with just the three women, the cooperative now has twenty members. And for Marie to be included in this book took the affirmative vote of all the women. Marie was adamant that all should be in agreement.

There are no stars in the Nawoitorong Women's Cooperative, although it is clear that Marie is the forceful, determined leader, a bridge between traditional Turkana women and the younger, more modern women. Members of both groups, because of their differing viewpoints, often hold up projects until they sit down with Marie and work out a solution that is mutually beneficial to the women and to the development of the cooperative. For instance, the bakery building,

which now also includes a store and an accounting office, was built by the women themselves from their brickworks located about a quarter of a mile away. But the cooperative's bricks are merely sun-hardened mud, and in the rainy season they often simply melt back into the ground. So the group is looking for a way to raise the funds to build a shelter for the bricks in order to keep them dry. Part of their clever solution is to educate some of their members in carpentry and plumbing at the polytechnic across town.

Also, although the bakery, store, and accounting office have a thatched roof that protects the mud walls from the rain, the posts that hold up the roof have been attacked by termites. The women have solved the problem by coating the posts with costly diesel oil. And each new project usually poses a new technological problem, which the women's group doggedly attacks.

In the meantime, it's business as usual, and the women arrive at the bakery at dawn and get down to work. Energetically kneading great piles of dough and slinging flour here and there, the women gossip as their small children play around their ankles. Thirty yards away, in front of the bakery, children of preschool age are taught by a young missionary woman who will serve them a hot lunch of maize and beans cooked on an open fire nearby.

In the back of the bakery the women have hand-dug trenches that hold new pipes leading to the Lodwar water line that provide tapwater for the enterprise. From their own tank, they sell water for twenty cents a *debe* can — half the cost of water in town. For the women living in the little village surrounding the bakery, the cooperative's water presents not only a savings in money but in time and physical exhaustion as they have previously had to carry forty-pound *debe* cans full of water on their heads the 3 1/2 kilometres (or 2 miles) from town.

The group's compound is growing into a bona-fide business centre, which now includes the bakery, the preschool, the accounting office, the brickworks, the waterworks, and the attached *duka*, or shop. The latter is a windfall project established almost by accident. When a week-long teachers' seminar was held in Lodwar, the women of the cooperative decided to undertake the catering. Marie, dynamic and organized, planned every menu for the entire week of the seminar; at sixty shillings per person per day, the venture was not only a tasty bargain for the teachers, but cost effective for the women's group. At the end of the week, the women found that they had earned quite a tidy sum. With foresight they voted not to pocket the money, but to start a shop that sells everything from the bakery's goods to toothpaste. So, unexpectedly, the women's group now has a thriving store as well as a thriving catering business.

The rapid growth of the catering business has taxed Marie's already limited time with planning and creating new menus. These include not only meals, but teas as well. She is a natural cook, devising her own dishes with the slim pickings of herbs and spices available in Lodwar. Yet she has created an astonishingly good meat dish and a beautifully light fish curry with what she has on hand. Her Lemon Twist Cake (page 112) is a reflection of her first and early love, the bakery.

Marie's catering menu bears no resemblance to the nomadic diet. She has mastered a cooking style that is as foreign to her indigenous style of cooking as Chinese is to Italian. For instance, in a traditional nomadic family, the women prepare all the blood and milk foods. The men — out herding the cattle, goats, and camels — prepare the meat. A typical day for the nomad begins in the *aui* with a meal of milk and blood. The men drink the blood and the milk mixed fresh, but the women prefer to cook the blood until dark and thick, adding milk and ghee until the whole concoction is the consistency of butter when cooled. While in the bush during the day the men might roast a whole camel, cow, goat, or the occasional donkey, neatly singeing off the animal's hair in the first roaring inferno of their cooking fire. Later they will bring back leftover roasted meat to the family when they return home in the evening. Dinner might be the meat, fresh or soured milk, or blood and milk mixed.

So Marie, at her young age and only a scant generation away from the sparse nomadic way of life, has adopted not only a new way to hustle, but is blazing a culinary trail of her own with an enviable firmness that often borders on quiet ferocity. For the settled Turkana women of the Nawoitorong Women's Cooperative, cooking has become big business. Marie and the group have had to work hard to keep one step ahead in their new business, pushing themselves to compete with the lodges and other caterers in Lodwar while running all their other enterprises. But Marie has adjusted to the new demands with a vigour, toughness, and intelligence that will hold the Nawoitorong Women's Cooperative together long after outside development teams have moved on.

Roasted Leg of Lamb or Goat

1 4- to 5-pound leg of lamb or goat
5 garlic cloves
1/2 cup soy sauce
2 tablespoons corn oil
1 teaspoon dried rosemary
Pinch salt
Pinch ground black pepper

Score the lamb or goat (Marie uses goat exclusively), and insert the garlic cloves in the meat. Mix the remaining ingredients and rub the meat thoroughly with this marinade. Let stand for several hours.

Roast in an oven heated to 375°F. for 30 minutes per pound. Brush often with the marinade and pan drippings. Add a little water to the drippings if necessary. (If roasting on a spit or barbecueing on a grill, simply brush the lamb often with the marinade.) Serves 8 to 10

Savoury Fish Curry

1 pound dried tilapia, or 1 pound fresh tilapia
or other firm white fish
2 medium onions, chopped
2 medium tomatoes, chopped
2 tablespoons vegetable oil
Pinch ground turmeric
Pinch ground coriander
Pinch ground cumin
4 cardamom pods, husked and crushed
1 cinnamon stick, crushed
1/2 teaspoon finely chopped green chili peppers, or 1/2 teaspoon
ground red (cayenne) pepper
1 cup water

If using dried fish, soak it in water to cover for 1 hour. Drain, reserving the water. Cut fresh or reconstituted fish into large pieces.

Fry the onions and tomatoes in oil until they form a thick paste. Add all the spices, fish, and water (use the reserved soaking water if available), and simmer for 30 minutes. Serve with rice. Serves 2

Lemon Twist Cake

4 ounces butter
1 ounce sugar
1 large egg, beaten
2 fluid ounces (4 to 5 tablespoons) milk
Juice of 2 small lemons
1/2 teaspoon baking powder
6 ounces all-purpose flour
Icing (confectioner's) sugar

Beat the butter and sugar together until pale and creamy. Beat in the egg, milk, and juice from 1 lemon. Sift the baking powder and flour together and fold into the butter mixture until well mixed.

Turn onto a well-floured surface. Divide the dough in two and roll each portion into a long sausage shape. Twist the two pieces together, moistening the dough at each end so that the pieces do not separate during baking.

Place carefully on a greased baking sheet and bake in a hot (375°F.) oven for 20 to 25 minutes, or until a pale golden colour. When the cake has cooled, mix the juice of the second lemon with enough sifted icing sugar to make a thin icing and spread it over the cake. Serves 6 to 8 as a teatime snack

12

Peter Kimanzi

*P*eter Kimanzi is a hard man to overlook. After all, the Hapa-Hapa Restaurant in Lamu is the best place to eat and Peter is the cook. The restaurant is newly owned and operated by four shrewd brothers from Nairobi; the first and smartest thing they did was hire Peter.

Peter, a Kamba from Kitui, was born far from the coast and certainly very far from the tiny island of Lamu, which lies nearly off the southernmost tip of Somalia. He finished Form IV (high school) and headed straight for a lodge situated on romantic Manda Island, a couple of hours by dhow from Lamu, where he waited tables and lived quite happily until his natural talent sent him straight to Utalii College, a hotel-management school near Nairobi. There he took a three-month crash course in cooking, landed back on the coast at Malindi, and from Malindi travelled on to Lamu, where his reputation had already preceded him.

Even though he is from up-country, the coast, oddly enough, is Peter's place. Freewheeling, hard-working, and charismatic, he stands out by a mile on this sleepy little island. When asked why he wasn't in Nairobi, where his talents would hitch him right to the top, his response was, "Nairobi disturbs me. Too many people." Obviously not wishing to be swallowed whole in the big city, he prefers to luxuriate in his not-so-minor notoriety right here on this small, remote island.

I met Peter on my first night in Lamu, when my companions and I were directed by just about everyone to eat at the Hapa-Hapa. At the time, Peter was waiting tables. I didn't want the raw vegetable salad and asked my waiter what other vegetable dish was on the menu. He stared into space for what seemed like ages; then he turned to me and quietly asked, "What do you want?" "Well," said I, not expecting much, "I'd like some cooked vegetables." "I'll make you some," he said simply. Just what was the waiter going to cook? I wondered, somewhat incredulously. The question was in my doubting eye, even if I dared not ask it in the face of his deadpan certainty. Letting me dangle a bit, he then looked me directly in the eye, and with a sudden, impish grin, said, "I'm the cook."

Peter brought me a vegetable dish, created on the spot, that ever after has been a favourite of the group I was with. From that moment on, we were hooked on Peter. I later found out that all he did was open a can of mixed vegetables and a can of beans, add 1 fresh tomato and 1 egg yolk, and drench it all in garlic and oil. To make Peter's vegetable dish from scratch is just as simple: For 2 to 4 people, boil 2 peeled, cubed potatoes, 4 chopped carrots, and 1/4 cup peas. Cook until all are tender, drain well, add 1 cup cooked green beans, and set aside. Then, in 1 tablespoon oil fry 1 chopped onion and 1 teaspoon freshly chopped garlic until the garlic is golden and the onions are clear. Add 1 chopped tomato to the onions and garlic and fry until a thick paste forms. Add the vegetables and mash all together gently until the vegetables are well blended with the tomato mixture. Now stir in the yolks of 2 eggs. Cook until the eggs are nearly done — not too long, just a minute or two — stirring constantly. Turn the steamy-hot concoction out onto a platter and serve with grilled fish.

Peter also makes a variation. In a little oil over high heat, he stir-fries fresh vegetables such as grated carrots, mushrooms, and chopped spinach along with 1 tablespoon garlic, 1 chopped onion, 1 lightly beaten egg, and 1 cup shredded crabmeat. He serves all his dishes with rice cooked in coconut milk (page 74; see pages 69–70 and 90 for instructions about extracting coconut milk).

Peter is a man of few words, always seemingly laid back, both literally and figuratively, but if you stick around long enough, you realize that his mind is on overdrive, always thinking about the best way to free himself for the important things, like creating his famous main dishes, including his Seafood Lasagne (page 120). For instance, he has taught his staff to make what he calls "*jua kali*" pasta, which frees him up to mother along the sauce. When Peter tackles the pasta himself, he beats 3 whole eggs together with 2 to 2 1/2 cups flour to make a soft, elastic, but not sticky dough. After kneading it, he rolls the dough into a 14-inch round, cuts the round into strips and rolls each strip very thinly, generously sprinkling with flour from time to

time. He continues to roll each strip of dough repeatedly until it is paper thin and measures 4 inches by 10 inches. Next, he carefully trims the edges to make the strips uniform. He drops each strip into boiling water for a minute or two, then very gently transfers each strip to a large plastic bucket of cold water, where he carefully "washes" the strips and drapes them over the edges of the bucket to drain until ready to use in the lasagne

Peter's utensils and kitchen are as unconventional as Peter himself. He cavalierly uses a flat ladle to measure his herbs and spices. Even though the ladle serves up an approximate 3 or 4 tablespoons, his recipes nevertheless turn out perfectly. He has only one or two knives — all-purpose utensils used for chopping, carving, peeling, scaling and opening cans, and he uses plastic buckets to do everything from soaking his pasta to mixing his Lobster Thermidor. Because of his heavy and constant use of garlic, his favourite undersize and overworked mortar and pestle, coming apart at the seams, is always leaking juice. Without his favourite utensils, no matter how bent or worn, Peter might be at a momentary loss. But he is anything but sentimental and if they finally become redundant, they would be replaced quickly by something as handy and as unconventional but no less effective.

His kitchen is the basement floor of the Hapa-Hapa Guest House, which was once the home of a wealthy Lamu family. The three rooms of the kitchen were storerooms, but Peter has handily converted them to suit his needs. The first room holds two truck-size freezers, a mess of potatoes, bunches of bananas, and little else. The main room holds a variety of tables for chopping, slicing, pounding, filleting, mixing, and everything else. The tables hold a variety of gas burners for cooking rice, chips, sauces, and curries. In one corner of the room, standing in pristine splendour, is a cooker that Peter uses almost exclusively for grilling his Lobster Thermidor and heating to bubbling the cheese smothering his Seafood and Mushroom Pizza (page 121).

In the third room, a large, red-hot barbecue is kept stoked all day to keep the tea-kettle bubbling and to grill great slabs of fresh tuna and shark, which are lunch and dinner favourites. At the other end of this room stands a sink of steaming hot water for washing dishes; a trench cut into the slightly slanted floor takes the soapy water away to the street. All Lamu kitchens work on this principle.

It is in this polyglot of rooms — hot and steamy but redolent with the perfection of his choice of herbs, sizzled garlic, and roasting fish

— that Peter spends half his time. He's a strong man, the kind of cook who opens cans with knives and husks and crushes cardamom between his bare hands. He has an unerring eye for the smallest detail — the odd thing out of place — missing nothing and running a tight ship while looking for all the world as if he had other things on his mind — until he goes into action to make his Lobster Thermidor (page 118). Then the whole kitchen jumps. The rest of the time he markets, waits tables, chats up the customers, drops into Petley's bar before lunch for a rare beer, and finally closes down the disco after hours.

Peter's Thermidor must be ordered a day in advance so that he can be sure to get a live lobster for you. You get the whole thing — not just half, or half of a half, or a tail, or half a tail, but the whole lobster. Although this dish bursting with garlic and herbs is my favourite, Peter's favourite is his Seafood and Mushroom Pizza.

Made for only two, the pizza is so rich that it will easily stretch to a meal for four. Peter never stints on ingredients, and the pizza is overflowing with tomatoes, fish, spices, and garlic. Peter is always generous in his portions and his generosity more than pays off; the Hapa-Hapa Restaurant is always packed. But such generosity isn't easy because the restaurant is island-bound. Most staples must be shipped in and are very expensive — everything except for the fish. Peter's main market is the sea, which gives him its treasures at rock-bottom prices.

Peter works hard for twelve hours a day. The Hapa-Hapa Restaurant is his job, his home, and his playground. In addition, he is the tireless promoter of the bed-and-breakfast guest house behind the restaurant that the brothers have remodelled. Of course, for breakfast guests are treated to Peter's full menu, which includes his wonderful banana pancakes, large bowls of fresh fruit, omelets, and, as he would say, "anything you want!"

Lobster Thermidor

4 large lobsters (at least 3 pounds), simmered in salted water
for 15 to 20 minutes
2 tablespoons crushed garlic
2 teaspoons dried marjoram
2 teaspoons dried rosemary
2 teaspoons dried oregano
2 teaspoons dried basil
2 teaspoons ground black pepper
Salt to taste
3 cups Peter's White Sauce (recipe follows)
2 large egg yolks
2 tablespoons fresh lime juice
1 cup grated cheese

Split the cooked, cooled lobsters in half lengthwise with a sharp knife. Open out the two halves of each lobster and discard the stomach sacs, the dark intestinal canals, and the gills. Retain the creamy livers and corals, if present, chop, and save for the sauce. Remove the meat from the tails and clean the shells.

Coarsely chop the lobster meat and place in a bowl. Add the garlic, herbs and seasonings, and reserved liver and corals, and mix well with the white sauce. Blend in the egg yolks. Finally, add the lime juice and mix all together very well.

Fill each shell (8 halves) with the mixture. Sprinkle cheese over the tops and grill for approximately 10 minutes, or until the cheese is bubbling and lightly browned. Serves 4

Peter's White Sauce

3 ounces butter
3 ounces all-purpose flour
3 cups (24 fluid ounces) milk
2 cups (16 fluid ounces) water

Melt the butter in a heavy saucepan. Stir in the flour and cook over low heat for 2 to 3 minutes, stirring with a wooden spoon. Gradually add the milk and then the water (Peter's combination of milk and water is a trick that keeps the white sauce light), stirring constantly to keep the sauce smooth. Continue stirring until the mixture comes to a boil and thickens. Makes 3 to 4 cups

Seafood Lasagne

1 cup vegetable oil
3 tablespoons finely chopped garlic
5 pounds ripe tomatoes, grated (see page 73)
2 teaspoons dried marjoram
2 teaspoons dried oregano
2 teaspoons dried rosemary
2 teaspoons ground black pepper
3 cups tuna stock (see Note)
2 cups *each* cooked chopped crab, lobster, prawns, and tuna
Salt
White sauce (see Note)
24 strips *Jua Kali* Pasta (page 114–115) or packaged lasagne
noodles, boiled in salted water until tender
1 cup grated cheese

In the oil fry the garlic and grated tomatoes. Add the marjoram, oregano, rosemary, and black pepper. Cook down until thick. Add the tuna stock and continue cooking for 30 minutes, or until the sauce thickens again. Add all the cooked fish and salt to taste. Simmer together for about 5 minutes.

Mix together 1 1/2 cups of the red sauce and 1/2 cup of the white sauce. Spread half the mixture in the bottom of a 10-inch square baking pan and cover with a layer of lasagne noodles. Spread 1 cup of the white sauce over the pasta and cover with more noodles. Top with 2 cups of the red sauce, followed by the remaining pasta and the remaining mixture of sauces. Sprinkle the cheese evenly over the top.

Bake in a 450°F. oven for about 15 minutes, or until the cheese is bubbling. Remove the lasagne from the oven, cool slightly, and cut into 2 1/2-inch squares. Serves 16

Note: To make tuna stock, simmer tuna head, tail, or bones in 2 quarts water for 20 to 30 minutes. Strain and use as desired.

For the white sauce, follow the method for Peter's White Sauce (page 119), but use 2 ounces butter, 2 ounces flour, and 3 cups milk, omitting the water.

Seafood and Mushroom Pizza

1 cup toasted bread crumbs
1 large egg, beaten
1 tablespoon margarine, melted
1 tablespoon grated tomato
1 tablespoon vegetable oil
1 tablespoon finely chopped garlic
5 to 6 tomatoes, grated
1/2 teaspoon dried marjoram
1/2 teaspoon dried rosemary
1/2 teaspoon dried oregano
1/2 cup finely chopped mushrooms
3/4 cup *each* boiled tuna, crab, lobster, and prawns (or any 3-cup
combination of mixed seafood that includes prawns)
Salt
1/2 cup grated cheese

To make the crust, mix the first 3 ingredients and spread on the
bottom of a deep 6-inch round pan. Spread the 1 tablespoon grated
tomato over the crust and bake at 325°F. until light brown.

For the sauce, heat the oil and fry the garlic; add the tomatoes
and herbs and cook until the tomatoes are cooked down into a
thick paste. Add the mushrooms and seafood. Mix well together
and cook for several minutes. Add salt to taste. Turn onto the
baked crust. Top with grated cheese and cook under the grill until
the cheese is bubbling. Serves 2

Crab Curry for Twenty

3/4 cup vegetable oil
1 head garlic, peeled and finely minced
1/2 cup finely chopped green bell peppers
20 medium tomatoes (about 4 pounds), grated (see page 73)
20 cardamom pods, husked
2 to 3 sticks cinnamon, ground
1 teaspoon ground cloves
1 teaspoon ground cumin
2 teaspoons ground black pepper
2 teaspoons ground turmeric
3 cups water
10 fresh crabs
1 ounce butter
2 tablespoons crushed garlic
1 cup crab stock
Pinch of rosemary
3 to 4 tablespoons lime juice
Salt to taste

Heat oil and fry the garlic and the peppers. Add the tomatoes, cardamom, cinnamon, cloves, cumin, black pepper, and turmeric. Simmer for 20 minutes. Add 3 cups water and simmer for 1 hour longer.

Boil the crabs in salted water for 30 minutes. Reserve stock. Cool crabs, shell, and shred the meat, carefully removing any pieces of shell.

Melt the butter and gently fry the 2 tablespoons crushed garlic. Add the crab meat, 1 cup of the reserved stock, the rosemary, lime juice, and salt. Simmer for another 10 minutes, stirring frequently. Add to the tomato sauce and mix well. Serve with Coconut Rice (page 74). Serves 20

13

Philippa Corse

lthough Philippa Corse is every inch a fair-haired Englishwoman, she has the glow of the golden Kenyan countryside written all over her beautiful face. Her parents came to the Sotik area of western Kenya at the tail end of an early settlement scheme, and it was in this remote farming district that Philippa was born and raised.

After World War I, British officers were awarded land in the highlands of Kenya by the English Colonial Office. Arriving in Nairobi with great expectations, these officers found that the unsurveyed land being awarded by lottery was simply a square on an otherwise uncharted map. They had no idea whether the land was flat, had water, was lush and fertile, or was dry as a bone; they also had little idea that the local tribes on these blank squares were flourishing. With little knowledge or help from the Nairobi Administrative Office, they gamely travelled from Nairobi to Sotik by bullock cart, bringing their intrepid wives and children to this potentially hostile and unknown countryside.

In turn the wives brought their fine china and lacy tea gowns, not knowing that their first home would almost certainly be a tent. Until the land was cleared, the last priority was the construction of a house, which, when at last finished, was more often than not a mud-and-wattle thatched-roof hut with a hardened dried cow dung floor. The tea gowns were packed away, and floppy felt hats with double brims and flannel spine pads became standard additions to their wardrobes, since it was believed that the rays of the sun at high altitudes close to the equator would evaporate the fluids around the brain and spine. In the Naivasha area, even the sheep wore spine pads, and children especially were not allowed out of doors unless suited up for the rigours of equatorial living.

Few survived the early days between the turn of the century and the late thirties. More often than not, after arduously clearing the land the farmers found that disease wiped out their livestock, or that water supplies and streams were inadequate, or, worst of all, that after surmounting every kind of problem, a successfully harvested crop rotted because the journey to the railroad over rough country and washed out roads took too long. Those who did survive were not only tough and clever but above all lucky.

Toughened by adversity and stretches of loneliness in remote and foreign lands, delicate Englishwomen were transformed into adventurous and capable farm wives able to tackle any crisis, from sewing on a farmer's severed thumb to shooting lions. But not all was wattle and daub, and eventually a hybrid concoction of English traditions and local custom took root as homes, gardens and small communities were created out of the African bush. It was to this early settlement that Philippa's family came.

Philippa grew up among the survivors at a time when farm tracks already had been hacked out of the plains and hills, making access for motor vehicles possible — just barely. Because the roads more often than not were a quagmire of muddy potholes or, worse, rivers after the long rains, settlers all over Kenya became good judges of horseflesh for work as well as for pleasure, and the traditionally English pastimes of horse racing and polo gave rise to stylish, if decidedly homespun, racecourses and polo fields stretching from Nairobi to Nanyuki. Philippa, like so many others, became a fine horsewoman out of the necessity of simply getting around the farm.

Reality was always colouring young Philippa's dreams. Her earliest memories, formed as she lay awake at night listening to the rustle of leather shields and the rhythmic thump of bare feet as warring tribes criss-crossed the family farm, were the settler's version of English fairy tales. Her make-believe world was all too excitingly real.

Yet every morning she awakened to mundane farm chores and hundreds of crises that had to be imaginatively solved. All over Kenya, English settlers settled down to making sense of their unbelieving eyes, dragging their traditions along with them, merging them with African customs where they fit, and finding their own solutions that in the end had little to do with England, other than where to place the multitude of silver knives and forks at the well-

laid table that to this day remains quaintly a part of their everyday lives.

In her early twenties, Philippa met George Corse, a Scotsman from the Orkney Islands who had been employed to plant and manage a tea estate in Kericho, a town not far from Sotik as the crow flies. He stayed on and married Philippa, who was now headmistress of a school in Nairobi. Together they have enjoyed a life filled with adventure, and there is hardly a part of Kenya's varied countryside they haven't travelled with their safari wagon, tent, and three children. So when her eldest daughter told Philippa that she wanted to marry a young English businessman at Christmas and that there would be forty-five guests coming on safari, no one was fazed, least of all Philippa. With her sunny smile and unflappable love of a good challenge born from the rigours of her early farming years, she immediately started organizing a tented safari high in the Chyulu Hills above Tsavo looking toward Mount Kilimanjaro.

Although the Chyulu Hills are but a ripple in Mount Kilimanjaro's wake, they are nevertheless inaccessible and rugged. Every morsel of food and every drop of water for drinking, washing, and cooking had to be carted up a steep, narrow escarpment road. Water tanks, tents, seating, tables, lighting, showers, bedding, cooking and serving utensils, decorations, and Christmas stockings were dragged up the rocky road, not in bullock carts but in a convoy of four-wheel-drive vehicles, which may or may not have been quicker. But once they reached the summit, the beautiful Kenyan landscape — its peace and quiet disturbed only by a bird's song — soothed the dusty travellers, along with a warm campfire, sundowners, and the laughter of the close friendships that flourish on safari.

Throughout three days of countless meals and endless teas, the guests, with dedication, kept the fires burning. Everyone got into the act of collecting supplies of wood for the meal preparations, which culminated in a rollickingly hearty English Christmas dinner. On Christmas Day, in order to accommodate nine large *sufuria*, a 7-foot-long, 2 1/2-foot-wide, and 1 1/2-foot-deep cooking pit had to be dug. The fire was lit two hours in advance of the cooking time, then allowed to burn down to a fine, hot glow of ash and embers. Two gridirons were suspended across the width of the trench to support the *sufuria* used to cook the vegetables and ham. Each end of the trench was heaped with embers for turkeys, which were wrapped in foil and placed in large *sufuria* with tightly fitted lids. Hot ashes were

126

then packed around the *sufuria* and replenished for the two and one half hours it took to cook the birds.

Although the meal was cooked at the campsite, the Christmas pudding was prepared months in advance and reheated on Christmas Day. An English housewife's reputation stands or falls on her Christmas pudding, and it must be cooked at least one month before Christmas, although often a year ahead is preferred. Ritual accompanies almost every step of the preparations, as superstition hangs on the coins that are covered in foil and cooked into the pudding. As the coins are added to the uncooked pudding mixture, each family member stirs the pudding three times, eats a spoonful, and makes a silent wish. At the Christmas dinner, the lucky person who gets more than one coin can expect a prosperous year. The result is that after everyone has finished greedily digging around in the pudding for the treasure, the only evidence of the cook's reputation left on the plate is a piled rubble of crumbs.

When the Christmas pudding was brought flaming to the guests on the Corses' safari, it signalled a brilliant climax to the Christmas season, but this safari also signalled the end of weeks of wedding preparations and celebration. The incense of woodsmoke, the magical night sounds of the wild African bush, the flaming pudding, and contented family and friends are forever a memory for Philippa.

Christmas Dinner on Safari

Fresh Grapefruit with Peppermint Liqueur
Sugar-Coated Boiled Ham
Sausage Stuffing
Herb Stuffing
Stuffed Roast Turkey
Roasted Potatoes and Onions
Minted Peas
Parsleyed Carrots
Turkey Gravy
Loquat Jelly
Kei Apple Jelly
Christmas Pudding with Brandy Butter
Kenyan Nuts and Dates

Fresh Grapefruit with Peppermint Liqueur

1/2 grapefruit per person
Crème de menthe liqueur, or minced fresh mint leaves
tossed in honey

Halve the grapefruits and cut the flesh into segments. Sprinkle
with crème de menthe and leave to soak into the grapefruit for
about 1 hour. Alternatively, sprinkle with mint leaves tossed in
honey.

Sugar-Coated Boiled Ham

1 12-pound ham, soaked in water overnight
Beer
Water
2 teaspoons whole cloves
1 1/3 cups brown sugar

Drain the ham and place in a large *sufuria*. Cover the ham in a mixture of beer and water, and add 2/3 cup brown sugar and 1 teaspoon cloves. Cover the *sufuria*, place on a gridiron that has been suspended over a fire pit filled with hot coals, and cook approximately 3 hours, or about 20 minutes per pound. When done, move the *sufuria* to one side of the fire to keep hot.

Half an hour before serving time, remove the ham from the *sufuria*, pat dry with a cloth, stud the skin with 1 teaspoon cloves and coat liberally with the remaining brown sugar.

Place the ham fat side down on a sheet of aluminium foil spread over the grill. When the sugar is brown and bubbling and has begun to caramelize, remove the ham to a clean, dry *sufuria* to keep hot until ready to carve. Serves 12 to 15

Sausage Stuffing

1/2 pound pork sausage meat
1 large onion, chopped
1 cup white bread crumbs
1 teaspoon chopped fresh sage, or 1 teaspoon dried sage

Mix all the ingredients together and freeze if desired. Thaw before using. Makes enough to stuff 1 15-pound turkey

Herb Stuffing

3/4 cup boiling water
2 1/2 cups dry bread
2 teaspoons chopped fresh parsley
1 teaspoon fresh thyme, or large pinch dried thyme
1 teaspoon chopped fresh lemon balm, or
1 tablespoon grated lemon peel
1 teaspoon salt
2 tablespoons butter, melted
1/4 teaspoon ground black pepper
1 cup finely chopped celery

Pour boiling water over the bread and let stand for 15 minutes.
Squeeze out as much water as possible. Add all the other
ingredients to the bread and mix well. Freeze if making in advance
and thaw before using. Makes enough to stuff 1 15-pound turkey

Stuffed Roast Turkey

1 15-pound turkey hen
Sausage Stuffing (page 129)
Herb Stuffing (page 130)
Vegetable oil
Ground black pepper

Remove giblets and set aside for gravy. Stuff the neck cavity with
Sausage Stuffing. Cover with neck skin secured with wooden
toothpicks. Stuff the tail cavity with Herb Stuffing.

Rub the bird liberally with cooking oil and pepper. Wrap in
aluminium foil and place in a *sufuria* just large enough to hold the
bird. (If cooking for a large crowd, it's better to cook more than one
bird in each pot to maintain an even heat.) Cover with a tight-
fitting lid and settle the *sufuria* securely in a bed of hot embers. The
pot should be loosely surrounded by embers, and regularly
replaced as needed. Cook 2 1/2 to 3 hours, or until the juices run
clear when the thigh is pierced with a skewer.

Twenty minutes before serving, remove the bird from the foil,
reserving the juices, and wrap in a tea cloth wrung out in boiling
water. Leave in a warm place until ready to carve. This makes the
flesh firmer and easier to carve. Serves 10 to 12

Roasted Potatoes and Onions

Boil for 10 minutes 1 pound peeled onions and 2 pounds peeled potatoes per turkey. Drain and make a cross-cut through the centre of each onion. About 1 hour before the bird is done, place the onions and potatoes in the *sufuria* around the turkey so that the vegetables can cook in the sizzling fat. Turn once. Drain well before serving. Serves 10 to 12

Minted Peas

2 pounds shelled green peas
Salt
1/4 cup chopped fresh mint leaves

Cover the peas with salted water, bring to a boil, cover the pot, and cook 10 minutes. Add the mint leaves and cook 5 minutes longer. Drain and serve. Serves 10 to 12

Parsleyed Carrots

2 pounds carrots, scraped and sliced
Salt
2 tablespoons brown sugar
2 tablespoons chopped fresh parsley
4 tablespoons butter, melted

Cover the carrots with salted water and add the brown sugar. Cook over medium heat for 20 minutes. Before serving, drain the carrots, add the parsley and melted butter, toss, and coat the carrots well. Serves 10 to 12

Turkey Gravy

Simply cover the reserved turkey giblets with cold water, bring to a boil, and simmer for 30 minutes to make a stock. Meanwhile, skim the fat from the *sufuria* in which the turkey was roasted, retaining all the juices and brown bits. Add 1 tablespoon flour to the *sufuria* and stir into the juices. Brown the flour over the fire, stirring all the time and taking care that it does not burn. Add a generous pint of giblet stock. Bring to a boil, stirring, to thicken the gravy. Strain into a hot jug or sauce boat.

Loquat Jelly

Make this when the fruit is in season. Wash and cut up any quantity of fruit available. Remove all the seeds, as these are poisonous when cooked. Put fruit in a saucepan with a little grated lemon rind. Barely cover with water and simmer until the fruit is reduced to a pulp. Pour into a thick, clean muslin bag and hang up to drain over a basin overnight. Measure the resulting liquid and add 1 pound of sugar to each pint of juice. Return to the saucepan and bring to a boil slowly to dissolve the sugar. Simmer carefully until a drop will jell on a cold plate. Pour into sterilized jars while still hot and cover when set. Keep in a cool, dry place.

Kei Apple Jelly

Choose ripe, unblemished fruit. (A few guavas will counteract the acidity of the kei apples.) Cut up the fruit, put it in a pan, and cover with water. Cook to a pulp and strain through a muslin bag as described in the recipe for Loquat Jelly (above). Measure, and add 1 1/4 pounds of sugar to each pint of juice obtained. Finish cooking and bottle as above.

Christmas Pudding

8 ounces self-raising flour
1 teaspoon salt
1/2 whole nutmeg, grated
1 teaspoon mixed spice (including allspice, cinnamon, and cloves)
12 ounces fresh white bread crumbs
12 ounces finely chopped beef suet
4 ounces brown sugar
1 pound currants
1 pound sultanas
2 pounds seedless raisins
4 ounces candied peel
2 tablespoons shredded cashews
1 large apple, grated
7 large eggs
Rind and juice of 1 orange
1/4 pint brandy or milk
1 silver charm or silver coin per person (plus 2 for luck), washed
and well wrapped in aluminium foil

Grease well 1 large and 2 small pudding basins. Have ready a large quantity of boiling water.

Continued

Christmas Pudding

Continued

Sift the flour, salt, and spices into a very large mixing bowl, then add all the remaining dry ingredients, including the apple, and mix well. Beat eggs until frothy and add orange rind, juice, and brandy or milk. Add this to the dry ingredients and stir well. Stir in the silver charms or coins. Turn the pudding mixture into the prepared basins and fill them almost to the top. Cover with a large round of buttered greaseproof paper and then with a layer of foil on top. Secure these coverings to the sides of the basins very tightly with string.

Set the pudding basins in large saucepans or *sufuria* and fill 2/3 full with boiling water. Cover with lids and boil the large pudding steadily for 6 hours (4 hours for the small ones), topping up the boiling water as necessary. Do not let the water stop boiling.

When cooked, carefully lift the basins out of the water and leave to cool. Remove the paper and foil and replace with fresh buttered greaseproof paper and foil. Store in a cool, dry cupboard for up to a year.

When ready to serve at Christmas on safari, boil again for a further 2 hours and turn out on a platter. Serve Brandy Butter (recipe follows) in a separate bowl. If desired, pour warmed brandy over the pudding, set alight, and bring to the table flaming. Serves 12

Brandy Butter

12 ounces butter
1 pound sifted icing (confectioner's) sugar
4 tablespoons brandy, or to taste

Cream the butter until soft, then gradually beat in the icing sugar. Beat in the brandy very thoroughly. Put in a plastic container and chill until ready to transport. Serve, softened, with Christmas Pudding (pages 134–135).

Make this a day or two before the safari and transport in a cold box or cooler.

14

P. S. S. Darbar

akuru is a busy railroad town in the heart of the Great Rift Valley. It is situated at the juncture of the roads that lead to Kisumu and Lake Victoria to the west, to Eldoret in the north, Nairobi in the south, and to Thomson's Falls and Nyeri in the east. The town is built flat out alongside the tracks and spills down to Lake Nakuru, which is mirror smooth and pink with flamingos. The old volcano, Menengai, flanks one side of the lake, while on the other golden plains rise up to meet the table-flat Mau escarpment. Nakuru is not just another stop along the line. It is geologically, historically, and economically in the centre of things. P. S. S. Darbar was raised in Nakuru town, and more than just a little of its hustle and bustle has rubbed off on him. He has been a grocer, a farmer, a hotelier, a cook, a caterer, and a restaurateur — and in turn also has played a large part in the town's success.

One of Darbar's early ventures was a shop that he stocked with imported European delicacies and with which he often experimented in his own kitchen. But this was before Darbar took cooking seriously. Cooking was purely a business proposition, and he bought a restaurant only to enhance his market, thus becoming his own customer. As supplier to his own restaurant, both businesses thrived.

Typical of Darbar's judgment, in picking his restaurant he chose a prime location in an airy corner of a two-storey building overlooking one of the busiest and most commercial intersections in town. At the time, his Oyster Shell Restaurant was a typical Kenyan up-country restaurant serving mostly roasted beef, chicken, chops, and chips, popular but hardly unique. Young and ambitious, he had no time to finetune a restaurant, as he was running a large hotel in town in addition to the market. Businessman before gourmet, he looked on The Oyster Shell and cooking as a second or even a third sideline to his other interests.

Then, through a series of transactions he sold The Oyster Shell Restaurant and found himself the owner of a farm outside Nakuru stocked with six hundred chickens and little else. Still the businessman, he sold his produce in and around Nakuru and Nairobi and woke up one day with ten thousand chickens, a staggering sideline. What to do with ten thousand chickens? True to his instincts, he turned his chicken farm into a frozen-foods business, employing twenty-five people in his expanding farm kitchen. He called his line of chicken pies and quiches Pio Pio Farms, *Pio Pio* being the sound his ten thousand chickens made and eventually the sound of music to his ears, as Pio Pio Farms became a runaway success.

After running a farm, a market, a hotel, a restaurant, and a line of frozen foods, Darbar now looked around for something more exciting, a new challenge requiring greater excellence. Closing a deal over a cup of coffee, he bought back his old restaurant and reopened The Oyster Shell with an entirely new menu that included his now famous Special Fish (page 145), Prawns *Piri-Piri* (page 144), Prawns *Masala* (page 143), and *Jira* Chicken *Masala* (page 142). His menu still includes Continental cooking — a popular steak-and-mushroom entrée and pastas — but his spicy fish, prawn, and chicken dishes, inspired by his rough, tough, fundamental, learn-it-the-hard-way years of experience, are to this day his most popular creations.

Across town, Darbar runs another successful restaurant, Kabeer, where he continues to serve much the same food he did during the early Oyster Shell days. Kabeer caters to the hurried business-lunch crowd, but The Oyster Shell, with fresh roses on the tables, white tablecloths, and soft music, is definitely for the world weary.

There are fancier restaurants laid out on bougainvillea-clad verandas, or rustic spas that overlook watering holes for wild animals, or Nairobi sophistication done up in damask and velvet. But The Oyster Shell, its windows curtained with billowing lace open to the town, has the ambience of a small Paris café. To sit at one of the small tables next to the open windows, where it is cool and the music is sweet, and watch Nakuru hustle is the best of all possible worlds. Alone, you can sit back and munch a few spicy samosas drenched in lime juice and wash them down with good Kenyan beer. Or you can meet a friend and dawdle over coffee and sweets. Or, because

Nakuru is more than 6,000 feet in altitude and you will find that you are always famished, you can order one of Darbar's overflowing plates of food. Either way, be assured that Darbar treats nibblers with as much care as trenchermen.

In The Oyster Shell's kitchen Darbar demands that his high standards be maintained by his staff. His boyish demeanor hides the soul of a demanding and precise cook. He pays close attention to just the right amounts, and you can always count on a dish being just what you ordered. But his choice of ingredients is anything but precise. He is not a stuffy cook or a conservative, play-it-safe-by-the-book sort of cook. For instance, his heavy use of caraway seeds is his trademark, unorthodox and controversial. But it's what makes his Special Fish so special, and there's no arguing with success.

Darbar shares his special dishes generously, unusual for a restaurateur in a small town where originality comes the hard way and cooking secrets are closely guarded. But then Darbar is a generous man, a charming man; he has lived in Nakuru all his life, and he works the town like a Hollywood agent works an opening premiere party. Good humoured and smiling, he hides a survivor's don't-bother-me-I-know-what-I'm-doing instinct. And if his restaurants went bust tomorrow, burned down and shut their doors, Darbar would rebuild better than ever with a new menu, inventing something new to titillate the Nakuru regulars. For instance, although Darbar has since moved on from the Oyster Shell Restaurant to give more of his time to Kabeer Restaurant, he has, with characteristic panache and innovation introduced Tandoori cooking, to the delight of Nakuru's diners. Not one to be moved by adversity, he's seen it all and has a zest for his business that reflects a professionalism earned by mastering every asset and capitalizing on every shred of luck he has made for himself.

Special Fish

2 pounds Nile perch or other white fish
All-purpose flour
Salt
6 tablespoons vegetable oil
1/2 teaspoon turmeric powder
1 tablespoon caraway seeds
1 teaspoon ground ginger
1 teaspoon crushed garlic
1 to 2 green chili peppers, chopped fine
2 medium onions, sliced
1 large green bell pepper, sliced
Juice of 2 lemons

Cut the fish into large pieces and sprinkle with flour seasoned with
a pinch of salt. Set aside. In a large frying pan, warm the oil over
medium heat. Add the turmeric and caraway seeds. Put the fish in
the pan and add the ginger, garlic, chilies, and salt to taste. Let the
fish fry gently for a few minutes and turn. Add the onion, bell
pepper, and lemon juice. Cover for a few moments, then remove
the lid and continue to fry everything together until the fish is
crispy. Serves 6

Jira Chicken *Masala*

1/4 cup vegetable oil
3 medium onions, finely chopped
10 whole cardamom pods, unhusked
10 whole cloves
5 cinnamon sticks
6 medium tomatoes, peeled and chopped
1 teaspoon ground turmeric
1 teaspoon *garam masala* (page 220)
1 teaspoon ground red (cayenne) pepper
2 teaspoons ground *jira* (cumin)
Salt
2 green chili peppers, finely chopped
1 teaspoon crushed fresh ginger
1 teaspoon crushed garlic
1/2 cup finely chopped fresh *dhania*
1 3-pound chicken, cut into pieces

Heat the oil in a large frying pan and add the onions, cardamom, cloves, and cinnamon sticks. Fry until the onions are brown. Add the tomatoes and stir. Add the turmeric, *garam masala*, red pepper, *jira*, salt, chilies, ginger, and garlic. Cook 5 minutes. Add the chicken pieces. Cook for 30 minutes longer. Add the *dhania* during the last 5 minutes. Stir frequently so that the vegetables do not stick to the pan. Serve with rice. Serves 4

Prawns *Masala*

4 tablespoons vegetable oil
3 medium onions, finely chopped
6 medium tomatoes, peeled and chopped
2 to 3 green chili peppers, finely chopped
1 teaspoon crushed fresh ginger
1 teaspoon crushed garlic
1 teaspoon ground turmeric
1 teaspoon ground *jira* (cumin)
1 teaspoon *garam masala* (page 220)
Juice of 2 small lemons
Pinch caraway seeds
2 pounds prawns or shrimp, shelled and cleaned
2 tablespoons finely chopped fresh *dhania*

Heat the oil and add the onions. Cook until the onions are brown.
Add the tomatoes, chilies, ginger, garlic, turmeric, *jira, garam masala*, lemon juice, and caraway seeds. Cook for 5 minutes, stirring constantly. Add 1/2 cup water if necessary to keep the *masala* from sticking. Add the prawns and cook for 10 minutes more. Sprinkle with *dhania* and serve immediately with rice or *chapati*. Serves 4

Prawns (or Chicken Wings) *Piri-Piri*

2 to 3 tablespoons vegetable oil
Pinch caraway seeds
1 teaspoon finely chopped fresh ginger
1 teaspoon crushed garlic
2 green chili peppers, finely chopped
1 pound large prawns or shrimp, shelled and cleaned,
or 12 chicken wings, boiled until tender and jointed
Pinch ground red (cayenne) pepper
Soy sauce

In a fairly large frying pan, heat the oil over medium heat. Add the caraway seeds, ginger, garlic, and chilies, and mix well together. Add the prawns or chicken wings. Stir all ingredients together well. Add the red pepper and sprinkle lavishly with soy sauce. Cover the pan and cook for 3 to 5 minutes. Serves 2 as a main course, or 4 to 6 as a starter

Special Fried Rice

4 cups water
Salt
2 cups rice, washed
4 tablespoons vegetable oil
1/2 medium onion, chopped
1 to 2 cups cubed uncooked fillet steak, mutton, chicken,
pork, fish, or prawns (shrimp)
2 large eggs
2 tablespoons soy sauce

Bring the water to a boil, then add salt to taste, rice and 1
tablespoon oil. Turn heat down and simmer until half the water
has evaporated, about 10 minutes. Turn down the heat, cover, and
cook until done.
Fry the onion briefly in the remaining oil and add the meat or
fish. Stir-fry all together for several minutes. Break the eggs into
the meat and stir. Add the soy sauce, then add the cooked rice. Mix
all together well and fry for a minute or two, stirring often.
Serves 4

Fruit with Chocolate Sauce

1/2 pawpaw (papaya), cubed
3 bananas, sliced
1/2 pineapple, cut into chunks
1 cup orange juice
1/3 cup powdered drinking chocolate or chocolate milk powder
Warm water
1 cup vanilla ice cream

Mix the fruit together and add the juice. Let stand several hours at room temperature, mixing and coating the fruit with the juice occasionally.

Make a light chocolate sauce by mixing the chocolate powder with a small amount of warm water. Divide the fruit and juice between 4 glass bowls. Add 1/4 cup ice cream to each bowl and top with 1 generous tablespoon of the chocolate sauce. Serves 4

15

Razia Khan

azia was raised in Moi's Bridge between Eldoret and Kitale in the lush highlands of the Uasin Gishu plateau. Her father ran a shop there. But when times got tough, he travelled to Lodwar to find work, leaving young Razia and her mother to run the shop. Barely a teenager during those days, she took care of the ordering, the accounting, the sales, and the customer pleasing. Although it was Razia's dream to go to the university, she got instead a heavy education in business that to this day makes her a formidable bargainer and an astute woman, clever and unafraid of risks. It was an education that was the making of Razia. She is philosophical about missing out on her studies, bears no grudge, has no regrets, and has made the best of all her opportunities.

Razia was married in an arranged marriage to a man seventeen years her senior who is well able to appreciate her charismatic, volcanic, yet kittenish personality. But the dominating aspect of Razia's character is her desire to help and please through her personal warmth and her love of cooking. Although she predominantly cooks Asian dishes, she creates lavishly, subjecting her patient and appreciative family to her newest inspiration, which they don't hesitate to comment on, sometimes improving the dish or sometimes prompting her to scrap it altogether. It doesn't faze Razia, whose ego is a practical one.

As Razia cooks, she moves quickly around the kitchen, flinging her matches on the floor, explaining, testing, observing alternatives, revealing where to shop for what, giving the pot a stir, explaining her herbs and spices — their uses in her cooking, as well as their medicinal purposes — pinching the chicken to see if it's done, or

carefully, almost tenderly, covering her rice with a wet cloth and placing it dead centre in her oven. She has immense energy, a quick wit, and no end of anecdotes and stories to accompany her cooking. If she is mercurial inside her kitchen, she is mercurially thorough outside when attacking a freshly killed chicken, stripping it nude within five minutes, and chopping it into seventeen edible pieces in the same amount of time. Did I mention that Razia also has a red belt in the martial art of tae-kwon-do?

Recently, although the town is bursting with close family members, it was Razia who held the month-long mourning rituals when her father passed away. Once a week friends and relatives from Mombasa to Moi's Bridge poured into Razia's spacious home for prayers followed by an elaborate afternoon tea. Prolific, inventive, cooking around the clock, Razia served a variety of teatime snacks that she rarely repeated during the month. Razia's tea is unspiced, just sweet, but her snacks are everything from freshly herbal, to sweetly spicy, to eye-wateringly hot. She served spicy meat patties, even spicier chick peas, an exotic, spicy green cake, hotter-than-hot lentil *bhajia*, hot maize cobs, and a variety of herbal and sweet flaky pastries, displaying her extensive knowledge of herbs and spices.

An all-purpose spice and herb pantry for the preparation of Asian dishes should include fresh ginger and garlic — pressed, frozen, chopped, or whatever, but not powdered. These are essential for Razia's dishes. Fresh *dhania* is also essential and can be grown like parsley, probably even more successfully. Next you'll need to have coriander, turmeric, *jira* or cumin, cloves, cinnamon, cardamom, and black pepper — each in whole and powdered forms. If you can't keep whole green chilies, have on hand plenty of ground red (cayenne) pepper. Grind and place in clean bottles with tight-fitting lids several *masala*s such as *garam masala* (page 220); *dhania jira*, which is a blend of coriander and cumin; and a tea *masala* that measures out to 1 teaspoon each ground cloves, cinnamon, and cardamom to 1/4 cup powdered ginger. Last of all, fresh or dried curry leaves are essential.

Razia's own store is formidable. Nothing is wasted in her house, and she keeps her many herbs and spices in any jar or bottle that she can lay her hands on, whether it be a peanut butter jar or a whisky bottle. Her store includes, in addition to the required staples, black, white, and green cardamom; whole dried chilies; caraway seed; nutmeg; mustard seed; rye seed; black cumin from Pakistan; sim sim;

fenugreek; dried whole paprika; thyme; sage; bay leaves; aniseed; all kinds of grains and nuts including pistachios, macadamias, and peanuts, rice flour, gram flour, wheat flour, maize meal, bread crumbs, corn flour, semolina, chick peas and chick pea meal, and black, green and red lentils (whole, halved and skinned); brown sugar; and a number of homemade chutneys, among them spicy-sweet mango.

Lentils are a family favourite. Razia puts them in soup, in curries, and in teatime *bhajia*. She uses skinned and halved lentils for soup and whole lentils for her curries. Served at lunch with whole-wheat *chapatis*, lentils are a complete meal. For her lentil curry, Razia soaks 1 cup whole lentils in water overnight. Several hours before the meal, drain the lentils, place them in a large saucepan, and cover with fresh water. Add 1 chopped onion, 1 teaspoon chopped fresh ginger, 1 teaspoon minced garlic, 1 teaspoon salt, 1 teaspoon ground turmeric, and 1/2 teaspoon ground red (cayenne) pepper. Chop fine 4 medium tomatoes and add them to the pot. Bring to a boil, reduce the heat, and simmer for 2 hours. Just before the lentils become tender, place 1/2 cup corn oil in another saucepan over medium heat. Add 1 teaspoon minced garlic and 1 teaspoon *dhania jira* (ground cumin and ground coriander mixed in equal proportions). If you want a hotter curry, add two split green chilies. Stir until the garlic is brown and add to the lentils. Continue simmering 20 to 30 minutes longer, or until the lentils are thickened and well cooked. Serve over rice. I made this lentil curry, which serves 4 to 6, in Cambridge, England, on a visit, and a young man asked for the recipe, saying, "I didn't know lentils were so good."

That's the beauty of Razia's cooking: not only is it delicious, but you want to try it for yourself. Cooking and teaching cooking come naturally to her; she makes it look so easy. And what's more, she has not the slightest hesitation in sharing her many cooking secrets. For instance, as a natural tenderizer, she skins, seeds, and grates several hard pawpaws, then spreads them in the sun to dry. Finally, she whirls the dried product in her coffee grinder and sprinkles the resulting coarse powder on meats.

Razia has another trick for skinning sacks of garlic in one go. She detaches the cloves from the heads, lightly rubs them with oil, and spreads them in the sun all day. At the end of the day, she wraps them in a soft towel and rubs them back and forth in the towel. The skins come right off. Then she purées the garlic in a blender, spreads the paste on a lightly greased baking sheet and freezes it for a half hour, cuts it into cubes, and returns the cubes to the freezer. When thoroughly frozen, she turns the cubes off the oiled sheet and puts the frozen cubes in a plastic bag or air-tight container. The result is that she always has fresh crushed garlic at her fingertips. She does the same with fresh ginger — mashing it, freezing it, cubing it, and returning the cubes to the freezer — and always has on hand fresh ginger for her curries.

Another trick for a smooth curry sauce is to halve tomatoes widthwise and rub them on a coarse-holed grater, leaving the skins for the dustbin. This is also very nice for soup. But Razia has an even cleaner, less fussy way of skinning tomatoes. She freezes them, and while still frozen, she easily skins them with her fingers. Then she thaws them and throws them into the pot.

Razia keeps fresh *dhania* and fresh spinach always handy in her freezer. She washes, drains, and chops them. When dry, Razia places them on a lightly oiled sheet and freezes them. Afterward, when they are thoroughly frozen, she puts them in separate plastic bags and replaces them in the freezer.

Razia also has medicinal uses for her herbs. Mint and aniseed are helpful for her children's tummy upsets. She dries the mint outside for 2 to 3 days and grinds the mint together with the aniseed to make a powder that can be taken with water. Or boil the mint leaves and aniseed in water for a tea or broth. Another concoction for indigestion is a mixture of aniseed, caraway, and sim sim in equal amounts, brewed or chewed. Yet another favourite remedy is a little cumin seed. After eating or any other time that you feel a bit queasy, chew well 1 teaspoon of cumin seed. It has a pleasant bitter-mint taste that is refreshing.

Razia's mother is the inspiration for her cooking and medicinal use of herbs, but Razia doubts that her daughter will take it up. Life is changing quickly in Kenya, and the old ways are disappearing. Razia's daughter will get the education that her mother always longed for, but it is hard to believe that she will ever be a match for her "uneducated" mother, who had perhaps the most valuable schooling there is: a hard, practical, fly-by-the-seat-of-your-pants type of education that has, for Razia, paid off.

Chicken with Spinach and Yoghurt

1 cup plain yoghurt
2 cups finely chopped spinach
1 cup finely chopped fresh *dhania*
1/2 cup finely chopped fresh mint
1 2-pound chicken, cut into pieces
1/2 cup vegetable oil
1 medium onion, grated
2 medium tomatoes, finely chopped
1 teaspoon crushed fresh garlic
1 teaspoon crushed fresh ginger
1 teaspoon ground red (cayenne) pepper
1 teaspoon ground coriander
1 teaspoon ground cumin
1 teaspoon ground turmeric
1 teaspoon salt

Combine the yoghurt, spinach, *dhania*, and mint. Coat the chicken well with the mixture and allow to marinate 1 hour.

Heat the oil, add the onion, and when brown, add the tomatoes, garlic, ginger, all the spices, and the salt. Then add the chicken, along with its green marinade. Cook slowly and simmer, stirring frequently, until you can see oil and the chicken is tender.
Serves 4 to 6

Potato *Masala*

8 medium potatoes
1 1/2 cups vegetable oil
1 teaspoon crushed garlic
1 large onion, finely chopped
4 medium tomatoes, finely chopped
1 teaspoon coriander seed
1 teaspoon cumin seed
1 teaspoon salt
Juice of 1 lemon
1 heaping teaspoon sugar

Peel the potatoes, cut in half lengthwise, and then cut lengthwise into quarters. Deep-fry the potatoes in 1 cup of the oil until golden brown. Drain and set aside.

In another pan, heat the remaining oil, and fry the garlic until brown. Add the onions, and fry until translucent. Add the tomatoes, coriander, cumin, and salt, and cook together for 5 minutes. Add the lemon juice and sugar and blend with the tomato mixture. Cook 5 more minutes, then add the potatoes. The dish can be served as soon as all the ingredients are mixed well together and heated through. Or put a lid on the pan, turn the heat down low, and serve when you are ready, up to 20 minutes later.
Serves 6 to 8

Biryani

3 cups rice
6 tablespoons vegetable oil
1 medium onion, grated
1/2 teaspoon *jira* (cumin) seed
6 cups water
3 teaspoons salt
4 medium onions, grated
1 cup corn oil
8 medium tomatoes, grated
1 cup plain yoghurt
1 teaspoon crushed fresh ginger
1 teaspoon crushed garlic
3 cinnamon sticks
6 whole cloves
1/2 teaspoon ground black pepper
6 cardamom pods, husked
Pinch salt
1 teaspoon ground red (cayenne) pepper
1 chicken, cut into large pieces
1 teaspoon ground coriander
1 teaspoon ground cumin
3 tablespoons chopped fresh *dhania*

Cover the rice with water and soak for several hours. Drain.

In a large saucepan, heat the oil and add the onion and cumin seed. When the onion is brown, add the water and bring to a boil. Add the salt and the rice. Boil until nearly dry, about 20 minutes. Turn the heat to low and cover for 5 to 6 minutes until completely dry. Keep warm while completing the dish.

Brown the onion in oil over medium heat. Add the tomatoes and cook until reduced by half. Set aside the onion and tomato mixture.

Continued

154

Biryani

Continued

In another pan, mix the yoghurt, ginger, garlic, cinnamon, cloves, black pepper, cardamom, salt, and red pepper. Place the chicken in a pan and cover with the yoghurt _masala_. Simmer 15 to 20 minutes until the chicken is tender. Add the tomatoes and onions and cook slowly until the mixture is thick, about 10 minutes longer. Add the coriander, cumin, and _dhania_ and mix thoroughly.

In a large baking dish or _sufuria_, layer half the rice, then all of the chicken, then the rest of the rice. Cover the dish or _sufuria_ and put in an oven heated to 300°F. 20 to 30 minutes. Serves 10

Sweet Rice

2 cups rice
4 1/2 cups water
Small pinch salt
1/4 teaspoon orange food colouring
4 tablespoons ghee or vegetable oil
8 cardamom pods, unhusked
1 1/2 cups sugar
1/4 cup sliced almonds
1/2 cup currants

Wash and rinse the rice several times in cold water. Bring 4 cups water to a boil, add the rice, salt, and food colouring, and turn the heat to low. When the rice is half done, after about 10 minutes, drain off the water, cover the pot, and set aside.

Heat the ghee or oil in a saucepan and add the cardamom and sugar with the remaining 1/2 cup water. Boil together until a thick syrup forms and add it to the rice in its pan, stirring well to ensure that the rice is well coated with the syrup.

Cover the pan and simmer the rice for another 10 minutes over low heat, or until the rice is al dente: done, but still firm to the bite. Stir in the almonds and currants.

In Razia's household, sweet rice is served with any main dish. But it is also delicious as a dessert. Divide the mixture between individual ramekins, dot with butter and spoon on some cream, and bake until warmed through. Serves 6 as a side dish, or more as a dessert

Khadi (Yoghurt Sauce)

2 cups plain yoghurt
2 tablespoons chick pea flour
6 cups water
2 tablespoons vegetable oil
1 tablespoon crushed garlic
1 tablespoon crushed fresh ginger
1/2 teaspoon mustard seed
2 medium tomatoes, finely chopped
2 green chili peppers, split
3 to 4 stems fresh curry leaves, or pinch dried
ground curry leaves (optional)

Mix the yoghurt with the chick pea flour and water and whip all together until well mixed.

Heat the oil and add the garlic, ginger, mustard seed, tomatoes, chilies, and curry leaves. Cook for about 5 minutes, then add to the yoghurt mixture. Simmer the yoghurt mixture for 60 minutes, or until thick, stirring frequently. Serve hot over any type of pilau. Makes about 3 cups

Breaded Curried Fish

1 pound tilapia fillets, or snapper or other firm white fish
1 cup flour or bread crumbs
Salt
Ground black pepper
1/2 cup vegetable oil
8 medium tomatoes, chopped
Juice of 1 medium lemon
2 tablespoons chopped curry leaves, or 1 tablespoon
dried ground curry leaves
1/2 teaspoon salt
1/2 teaspoon ground red (cayenne) pepper
1/4 teaspoon mustard seed
1/4 teaspoon cumin seed
1/2 teaspoon ground coriander
1/2 teaspoon ground cumin
3 tablespoons chopped fresh *dhania*

Dip the fish in flour or bread crumbs seasoned with salt and pepper. Fry the fish in 1/4 cup of the oil until golden brown and remove to a plate.

In another pan, heat the remaining 1/4 cup oil and fry the tomatoes, lemon juice, and all the other ingredients until a thick sauce forms. Add the fish to the sauce, and simmer for 5 minutes, covered. Serves 6

Lentil *Bhajia*

2 cups halved green lentils
2 green chili peppers, finely chopped
1 teaspoon crushed fresh ginger
1 teaspoon crushed garlic
1/2 teaspoon cumin seed
Pinch ground turmeric
Pinch salt
1/2 cup *dhania*, finely chopped
Vegetable oil

Cover the lentils with water and soak for 24 hours. Drain the lentils well for 30 minutes or more, and then squeeze "dry."

Chop or grind the lentils until fine. A pestle and mortar are preferable for maximum flavour. If grinding with a blender, add a little water so the machine will run smoothly. Do not overgrind, but keep the mixture a little coarse. Drain and squeeze dry.

Add all the other ingredients except the oil and mix well. Form balls of the mixture by the tablespoonful. Deep-fry in hot oil, turning often. Drain the *bhajia* and cool before serving. Serve a chutney on the side if you wish. Makes about 3 dozen

Spicy Picnic Meat Patties

4 slices bread, crusts trimmed
1/2 cup milk
1 pound minced beef
2 green chili peppers, finely chopped
1 teaspoon crushed garlic
1 teaspoon crushed fresh ginger
Pinch salt
1/2 teaspoon ground red (cayenne) pepper
1/4 teaspoon ground turmeric
1 teaspoon *garam masala* (page 220)
1 bunch *dhania*, finely chopped
2 tablespoons vegetable oil

Dip the bread in the milk and squeeze out the excess moisture. Set aside. Mix the beef with all the other ingredients except the oil. Add the bread and mix all together well, using your fingertips. Make small meat patties about 2 inches in diameter and 1/4 inch thick. Fry until golden brown in the oil. Drain and serve hot or cold as a teatime or picnic snack. Makes about 2 dozen

Corn-Cob Snacks

1/4 cup vegetable oil
10 medium tomatoes, chopped
Juice of 1 medium lemon
2 tablespoons chopped curry leaves, or 1 tablespoon
dried ground curry leaves
1 teaspoon ground red (cayenne) pepper
1/2 teaspoon ground mustard seed
1 1/2 teaspoons ground cumin
3 tablespoons finely chopped fresh *dhania*
1/2 teaspoon salt
5 ears maize or corn, cut into 2-inch rounds and boiled
in salted water

In the oil, fry the tomatoes together with the lemon juice, curry
leaves, ground red pepper, ground mustard seed, cumin, *dhania*,
and salt. Cook until the tomatoes form a thick sauce. Add the
precooked maize or corn. Simmer all together for 15 to 20 minutes
longer. Can be eaten hot or cold. Serves 6 to 8

161

Chick Peas in Light *Masala*

1 pound dried chick peas
2 medium onions, grated
3 tablespoons vegetable oil
1 heaped teaspoon crushed fresh ginger
1 heaped teaspoon crushed garlic
1 teaspoon ground cumin
1 teaspoon ground coriander
1 teaspoon ground red (cayenne) pepper
1 teaspoon salt
1/2 teaspoon ground black pepper
4 medium tomatoes, chopped
Juice of 1 lemon
2 teaspoons finely chopped fresh *dhania*

Soak the chick peas overnight in water to cover. Drain, cover again with water, and boil until tender, 2 to 3 hours. Drain and cool.

In a saucepan, fry the onions in the oil. Add the ginger, garlic, cumin, coriander, ground red pepper, salt, and black pepper. Stir all together, then add the tomatoes. Fry until the sauce becomes thick. Add the chick peas and the lemon juice, and mix all together well. Just before serving, add the *dhania*. These can be served hot or cold. Serves 10 to 12

Potato-Stuffed *Chapati*

1 pound potatoes, peeled, boiled and mashed
1 to 2 heaping tablespoons ground red (cayenne) pepper
1 heaping tablespoon salt
1 heaping teaspoon cumin seed
Juice of 1 lemon
1 cup *dhania*, chopped
1 recipe uncooked *chapati* dough (page 217)
All-purpose flour
Vegetable oil

Mix the potatoes and first 5 ingredients together well.

Pinch off an egg-size piece of *chapati* dough and roll it out to about 6 inches in diameter. Place a ball of the potato mixture the size of small orange in the middle. Wet the edges of the *chapati* and pull it up around the potato ball, covering it completely. Dip the ball in flour and roll out again to 6 inches in diameter.

Place on a hot *chapati* griddle, a heavy, flat pan without sides, or in a cast-iron frying pan. Over medium-high heat, cook about 30 seconds on each side. Brush a little oil on each side and cook until the *chapati* rises a bit, turning after 20 to 30 seconds and pressing the *chapati* into the pan with either a spatula or a pad of cloth. When the *chapati* is nicely browned, remove to a rack and drain. Repeat with remaining dough and potatoes. Potato-Stuffed *Chapati* are good hot or cold, and can be eaten immediately, put in the children's lunchboxes, or taken on picnics. Makes 12 to 15

Halwa

1 cup milk, scalded and cooled
1 1/2 cups water
1 large egg, beaten
10 cardamom pods, husked and crushed lightly
3/4 cup sugar
1 cup butter
1 cup semolina
1 tablespoon currants (optional)
6 slivered almonds (optional)

To the cooled milk add the water, egg, cardamom, and sugar. Set aside.

Melt the butter and stir in the semolina. The semolina-butter mixture will look a little dry in the pan. Add the milk mixture and continue stirring over medium heat until the mixture is quite thick and the butter is separating slightly, about 8 to 10 minutes. Stir in the currants and half the slivered almonds. Pour the *halwa* into an ungreased mould or pan. Sprinkle the rest of the slivered almonds over the top. Refrigerate and, when set, cut into squares. This makes a wonderful teatime snack. Or, in the morning, breakfast on fruit, a plain omelet, and *halwa*. If you're really serious about your *halwa*, serve it hot as a porridge. Serves 4

African Tea

1 cup water
1 teaspoon loose tea
3 cups milk
3 to 4 tablespoons sugar

Boil the water and add the tea. Boil for 3 to 5 minutes. Add the milk, bring back to a boil, and boil gently for 3 to 5 minutes. Add sugar to taste. Strain into a pot. Serves 2 to 4

Handwa Cake

1/2 cup chick pea flour
2/3 cup wheat flour
1 cup plain yoghurt
1 teaspoon crushed garlic
1 teaspoon crushed fresh ginger
1 teaspoon finely chopped fresh *dhania*
Pinch ground turmeric
1 tablespoon finely chopped fresh fenugreek, or 1 teaspoon
crushed fenugreek seed
1 teaspoon *jira* (cumin) seed, crushed
1/2 cup grated marrow (see Note)
2 small green chili peppers, crushed
1/2 cup vegetable oil
1/2 teaspoon small mustard seed
1 teaspoon sim sim seed

Soak the chick pea and wheat flour in the yoghurt. The mixture
will be soft and thick, like paste. Let stand overnight, then add the
garlic, ginger, *dhania*, turmeric, fenugreek, cumin, marrow, and
chilies. Mix all together well and place in an 8-inch loaf pan.

Heat the vegetable oil and when very hot, add the mustard and
sim sim seeds. Fry until the seeds just turn brown. Pour the oil and
seeds over the batter in the pan.

Bake in the oven at 350°F. for 20 to 30 minutes. Cool, slice, and
serve with hot, sweet African Tea (page 164). Makes 1 8-inch loaf

Note: If marrow is unavailable, substitute 2 peeled and grated potatoes to
which a pinch of bicarbonate of soda has been added.

Mango Chutney

3 large hard unripe mangoes, or 6 small ripe green mangoes
Salt
1 cup vegetable oil
3 dried red chili peppers
1 teaspoon ground *jira* (cumin)
8 whole cloves
3 small cinnamon sticks
1 teaspoon ground red (cayenne) pepper (optional)
2 cups sugar

If using the large, unripe mangoes, peel and grate them, sprinkle with 2 teaspoons salt, and allow to drain for at least 1 hour. Put in a cloth and squeeze dry.

If using the small, ripe mangoes, peel and grate. The resulting pulp will be somewhat watery, but draining is not necessary before continuing with the recipe.

In the oil, fry the dried chilies, cumin, cloves, cinnamon, and ground red pepper. Add the grated mango and the sugar. Cook, stirring frequently, until you can see oil rising to the top, about 30 minutes (15 to 20 minutes for the ripe mangoes). Add salt to taste and adjust sugar and chilies. Put in a clean jar and stir every now and then with a spoon. The chutney will keep for months.
Makes about 2 cups

16

Rebecca McDougall and Lydia Sungurar

*A*merican missionaries Rebecca McDougall and her husband, John, live in the small, forested village of Gatab high atop Mount Kulal, which rises out of the desert at the southeastern tip of Lake Turkana. Looking out through the vine-covered front doorway off her small, green-lacquered sitting room, Rebecca can see the entire southern end of the 200-mile-long lake, including South Island. Central Island is the breeding ground for the lake's crocodiles. North Island is uninhabitable, even for crocodiles. Perched on the cool, green, fertile mountainside, Rebecca's house is in serene contrast to the desolate, forbidding desert that lies at her feet, still and hot, at 108 degrees Fahreinheit in the shade. But in Gatab, on the mountain, the Samburu who have settled here after leaving the desert below are covered up against the chill. As for Rebecca, she is a one-woman oasis of bright, sunny cheer. Even though we draw up to her small house unexpectedly at dusk, she makes you believe that she has been waiting all day for your arrival. She is the type of woman who, once you have met her, even for a few days, will always be in your life somehow.

An American from the Southwest, Rebecca has had to adapt her tastes and cooking style to the very limited types of food grown on the slopes of the mountain. The few cherished spices of turmeric, ground red pepper, cinnamon, and cloves that she carefully and prudently uses are a reflection of the Boran tribesmen who mingle with the Rendille and Samburu in the Northern Frontier District of Kenya. Otherwise, she has to rely for supplies upon a plane that lands sporadically on a small landing strip nearby, as the road in and out of Gatab, and up and down the mountain, is no bigger than a cattle trail the width of one not-so-well-fed-cow, with a sheer drop of 2,000 feet on one side. And when visitors get over the shock of arriving safely up the mountain, they are left with the prospect of having to get down again. Once is definitely enough. So Rebecca relies on the quixotic timing of the small plane, which brings little more than the "staples" of sugar, Cokes, and cookies.

Rebecca's cuisine is understandably simple. The first night we arrived at her vine-smothered house, dinner was over, but we were offered great blue plastic mugs of steaming, milky-sweet African tea — and popcorn. It was typical of the Afro-Americana that Rebecca has combined in her customs of hospitality. After travelling all day across empty, apricot-coloured deserts; dry, white riverbeds; and the bleak, grey rubble of the town Kargi, which at the time was engulfed in a blinding, yellow-brown dust storm, we were grateful.

Breakfast was no less a matter of necessity being the mother of invention. Having no real taste for the local porridge, Rebecca settles for a Continental breakfast. Early, before anyone was awake, she baked a sugary, doughy cake flavoured with cubes of pawpaw that was as close to an American Danish pastry as she could get. In the cool, fresh, early light with the front door standing open to the unsullied morning air and the cloudless china-blue sky, the lake spread out below misted with shimmering heat, it was one of the nicest, if not one of the sweetest, breakfasts I've ever had.

In the mornings, after her husband leaves to help the villagers with various water and livestock projects, Rebecca doesn't have long to wait for the first Samburu women from the church to knock on her door. They come singly and in pairs, all with babies safely tucked into brightly coloured *kanga* and slung in front or in back. These settled Samburu women of the mountain have adopted Western dress and removed their only assets, the dowry of up to six pounds of beaded necklaces that are worn at all times and never removed unless sold. Now, comfortably clad for the cool mountain air, wrapping their sweaters around their shoulders, the women settle down to some lively gossip. Chatting in Swahili, Rebecca swaps stories with Kutumbee Sungurar, who has taken the Christian name Lydia and who happily tells us about her traditional Samburu wedding.

Early in the morning of Lydia's wedding day, her bridegroom

killed a cow at her father's house, which was then eaten at certain times of the day by various members of the community, depending upon their age and sex. Early on, the young women cooked their portions, mixed with a little sweet milk, in a clay pot that had been soaked with water. At nine in the morning, the older women roasted their shoulder portion over a fire. Between ten and eleven the men took the legs and ribs into the forest and roasted these pieces, while inside the house the bride drank milk and blood with her friends.

The feasting continued until the bride set up a wailing, a signal for the bridegroom to come and get her. Late in the evening, after feasting all day, the elders arrived at the house to present the pair to each other and to give them advice, gently admonishing them to get along with each other, blessing them, and wishing them many children and peace in their house. Lydia and her bridegroom stayed in her father's house for the first night, and the next morning, when all had gone well and the pair agreed that they were suited and happy with the arrangement, she left her father's house loaded down with household gifts from her clansmen and set off for her husband's home.

A reflection of Lydia's roots and the simplicity of life in Gatab among the Samburu is Lydia's choice of recipes to share. For instance, she tells Rebecca how to cook milk: "Put 2 cups milk in a pot. Boil. Remove from heat and cool. Drink." Boiling milk is traditional all over Kenya, whether it is for tea, making ghee, or for wedding ceremonies. Her next recipe is a reflection of intercultural communication within Kenya, especially with the Boran in the area: "Bring 2 cups of water to a boil. Add one cup rice until the water is gone." The following instructions reflect the transportation not only of new cooking ideas but of new staples (onions and salt): "If you have meat, onions, beef bouillon, 3 tablespoons oil, 1/2 teaspoon of salt, cook together before adding the water. Then add water, then rice, and cook until the water goes away. Don't stir!"

Lydia is especially proud of her egg recipe, since chickens are not indigenous among the Samburu, who are red meat eaters. "In a small bowl, crack 2 eggs. Scramble with a pinch of salt and 1/2 teaspoon of sugar. Cook in oiled skillet. You may add 3 tablespoons milk." Then she goes on: "For fancy eggs, cook with rice which has been boiled in beef stock. For fancier eggs, chop onion, tomatoes, and spinach, and cook until they smell good. Add boiled, diced potatoes. Add eggs and salt." I can detect some of Rebecca's influence in the traditional American desire to empty everything into one pot.

Lydia cooks *chapati*, *ugali*, and the ubiquitous Kenyan stew with meat, onions, *sukuma wiki*, and tomatoes. But she also cooks a nomad's goat soup similar to Richard Kisaro's (page 176–178), except that she uses salt instead of traditional roots and adds rice to the stock.

Rebecca's cuisine is no less simple and no less a reflection of her interaction with the Samburu of Mount Kulal. If she strives to keep her American fast-food traditions alive at these dizzying heights, she also often gives in to an impressive, innovative display of tribal cooking. For instance, she cooks a Kikuyu dish of *githeri*, a stew of beans and maize, with a mishmash of tribal custom, Asian spices, and leftovers from the fridge. She invents many such concoctions, which, if not *cordon bleu*, are farmhouse filling.

The simple life in Gatab is reflected in Rebecca's cooking and gives the best picture of life high atop the mountain, where she has attempted to mix and match her own traditions with Kenya's fresh, homegrown ingredients. For instance, the last evening we spent with Rebecca, she surprised us and put on a Tex-Mex-Afro feast of tacos made with her version of *chapati* filled with spicy minced meat and topped with avocado. Her *chapati* were closer to American flatbread; her meat was spiced with the ground red pepper that is sold by the Boran in the Marsabit market; and the avocado was pure Gatab.

After dinner, when it grew dark, Rebecca's house was filled with blanket-wrapped Samburu who sat in front of her warm fireplace, her green sitting room lit by the flare of the fire and by the blue-neon glow of a solar lamp. The eerie light flickered down her lavender halls, through the pink bathrooms and blue bedrooms and out the doors and windows, where the sunset could be seen, as colourful as Rebecca's crazy-quilt house. As the sun went down, a bank of black clouds was backlit ominously until the sun set behind the lake and caught the clouds on fire. The inferno ringed the ancient lake, and for a moment it seemed as though we were watching the beginning of time. Our only regret in the euphoria of the firelit glow was that tomorrow we would be zigzagging down the cow trail that slip-slides down Mount Kulal.

There is only one way to capture Rebecca's infectious, cheerful, informal essence as a person and as a cook, as well as her simple life on Mount Kulal, and that is to reproduce her recipes here as she wrote them to me in a letter. She ends her letter: "One day, perhaps, we shall meet again."

Rebecca McDougall's *Githeri*

"Wash 2 cups of red beans and 2 cups of maize. Put in a large pot and cover with water. Simmer, covered, until the water is gone, then add as much water again, and again. When that's gone, and the beans and maize are soft, mash together. In another pan, gently fry 2 small chopped onions on a low heat in oil. Add to bean and corn mixture. Add 1 cup water. Add 2 teaspoons curry powder [or if fresh spice is preferred, use a combination of 1/4 teaspoon ground turmeric and a pinch each of ground red (cayenne) pepper, cumin, coriander, cinnamon, and cloves] and 4 teaspoons beef stock. Simmer 1 hour. Eat! If you have potatoes or pumpkin, *sukuma wiki*, or cabbage, chop and sauté (fry gently in a little oil). Add to beans and maize when you add the onions. Cook 1/2 hour longer." Serves 6 to 8

Flatbread

"In a large bowl, put 2 cups water and add enough flour until stiff. Break off pieces of dough 1 tablespoon at a time and with a rolling pin, roll them into pancakes. Add 1/2 teaspoon oil and spread onto each as you roll it out. Roll up the pancake like a crêpe. Then coil into a flat ball; roll out again with a rolling pin and place on lightly greased hot skillet to fry. Turn once."

Papaya Delight

"Sauté diced green pawpaws in a bit of oil. Add water and sugar to make a syrup. Spice with cinnamon and cloves and serve on fried rice or with *ugali*. May also add onions."

Sautéed Salad

"Sauté in oil: celery, green onions, bell pepper, spinach, *sukuma wiki*, cabbage, beet greens, parsley, and a bit of sugar. Add: avocado slices, juice of 2 limes, pinch of salt and a dash of pepper."

Curried Pumpkin

"Cut a large pumpkin open. Peel. Cut into small pieces. Chop 2 medium onions. Sauté in 3 tablespoons oil. Add pumpkin and cover. Add 1 teaspoon curry powder [Again, Rebecca uses tinned curry powder, but if fresher flavours are preferred, try the combination of a pinch each of ground cinnamon, cloves and ginger; 3 cardamom pods, husked, seeded, and ground; 1/4 teaspoon ground turmeric and 3 whole black peppercorns, ground] and 2 teaspoons beef stock and cook over low heat for 1/2 hour. Add 1 1/4 cups water. Simmer 1/2 hour. When soft, eat."

17
Richard Kisaro

*T*he Chyulu Hills that lie across the plains from Mount Kilimanjaro are but a hiccup compared to the majestic shadow of the mountain that dominates the landscape, and the tough, brown-scrub plains that lie at its foot are but a tiny part of Maasailand, which stretches up out of Tanzania and into Kenya. Out on these colourless plains live the most colourful, most talked about, most written about, most researched, and most photographed tribe in Kenya. The Maasai, fierce, nomadic pastoralists, have pricked the imagination of the Western world ever since the British first tramped through their territory while building the Uganda Railway from Mombasa to Lake Victoria. Some of the research and legend have combined in speculations that the Maasai originated in northern Africa and have their roots in the Roman occupation and exploration of the continent. Brightly draped in red togas, they are graceful warriors with fine features and a self-confidence that stems from their mastery of the land.

Several generations ago, when Kenya became a focus of European expansion, many of the Maasai moved out of the plains and up into the rich and fertile Kilimanjaro foothills, where they became settled farmers. Richard Kisaro's father was just such a one, and he bought a 41-acre farm along with a wild, untouched forest, both of which today support a large extended family. Orphaned now, Richard is the head of the family and farms the land in various ways. He grows beans, *sukuma wiki*, and maize for family consumption and oranges and coffee as cash crops; he also grazes cattle and raises chickens. But Richard's greatest pride is the forest that produces roots for cooking, as well as for medicinal purposes.

Several years ago, Richard was paralysed in one leg. After one solid year of tests and treatments in and out of hospitals, and with no change, a neighbour suggested medicinal roots. For one week Richard boiled the recommended roots, blended the resulting tea with honey, and drank it twice a day. At the end of one week, Richard took his first faltering steps. Now he runs to town and back and walks without a limp. He is completely fit.

These same roots (including the *oltimigomi* root, which Richard told me makes warriors "hot," or fearless and courageous) were boiled for me in a Maasai goat soup. Feeling nineteen again after drinking Richard's goat soup, I believe in his roots and their power to heal.

The soup I was served is cooked by men only according to Maasai tradition, and it is eaten out in the bush while grazing cattle and goats. In fact, among the Maasai only men cook meat, however it is prepared. With grave humour, gentle concentration, a happy reverence, and great expectations, he set out to prepare the soup for me.

Early in the morning, Richard took me to the market in Loitokitok, where we visited the herbalist. Even though all the needed roots can be found in his forest, Richard decided to save time and buy them at the market. There were several herbalists, each with bunches of roots neatly stacked on a clean gunny sack laid carefully on the ground. And each bunch contained a sampling of several kinds of roots for anything from a cough to "not enough blood," which I interpreted as anaemia or some ailment that was characterized by a lack of energy.

While at the herbalist's Richard cordially began chatting with Aggrey sheke ole Mpario, a Maasai born in 1919 who had a thorough knowledge of the pile of roots that Richard bought for his soup. Although they were complete strangers, Richard invited Aggrey to accompany us back to his farm and help in the preparations, an invitation that Aggrey sheke ole Mpario solemnly and proudly accepted. It was apparent that the *mzee* was honoured to participate in the cooking of the soup, which gives an idea of its importance in the lives of the Maasai.

A whole goat is usually slaughtered in the morning, and the soup is eaten at noon or one o'clock. But today, only a large, fatty part of the back and rump is used. The soup was cooked in a *sufuria* over an open fire that was kept going within the traditional triangle of no more and no less than three stones. After the fire was laid and before the meat was added to the pot, Aggrey stripped the bark off a nearby

176

tree and flayed the meat against the fresh wood to break down the fat and tenderize the meat so it would cook faster. The meat was then placed in a large *sufuria* over the fire, which was constantly fed with three very long twigs, the fresh ends of which were inched into the fire to keep it going. After the meat had boiled for two or three hours, it was removed from the pot and hung on a tree to be eaten separately after the broth.

While the soup was cooking, the roots were covered with water and soaked in a small *sufuria*. Then, ashes were scraped to one side of the main fire and the roots were simmered in the ashes. The resulting tea or broth was a dark reddish brown and eventually gave the soup a nice colour. Before Richard added the root tea to the broth, Aggrey churned the broth with an *olkipire*, a stick fitted with a goat's vertebrae and whirled between the palms to mix in the fat. After Richard added the boiled root broth to the goat meat broth, Aggrey churned the whole concoction again with the *olkipire* until all was well blended. Now the soup was ready to drink.

The large *sufuria*ful of broth ordinarily would have been shared by only two men. (The Maasai are prodigious eaters and lovers of meat, fat, milk, and fresh blood. Richard can eat three and one-half pounds of meat in one sitting.) But since there were three of us, it was a full meal for me and a snack for them. They each quickly drank off three mugs apiece as I sipped my first. The broth was thick, heavily laced with fat, and both sweet and salty; it tasted very much like beef bouillon, even though no other seasoning than the roots was used.

As we sipped our broth, Aggrey told us in the Maa language the uses of the roots as Richard translated: "*Olkonyil* is good for women and joints [politeness dictated that I not question just how and why it is especially good for women]. It is a bitter root and found on the slopes of Kilimanjaro, not on the plains. It is also found in the Chyulu Hills. *Olkokola* is good for all the joints of the body. It is very bitter. It is for the blood and joints of older people. [Richard never tired of joking and laughing about the name of this root and its similarity to Coca-Cola, which is drunk prodigiously in Kenya.] *Oltimigomi* is good for warriors. It gives them energy and is good for the chest. The roots are bitter, but the stem of the tree is not. Both can be boiled in the soup, but it is not necessary. *Olasesiai* is a very sweet root and is used for soup only. It turns very red when boiled. *Olamuriak* is good for soup and is very sweet."

Richard and I later looked up the English equivalents for these roots in an incomplete dictionary of the Maa language. He worries that his children know only the Maa that he knows and feels that the language is dying out. Richard himself speaks fluent and flawless English. But when I checked with the National Museums of Kenya in Nairobi, the botanical names of the plants were easily available: *olkonyil* (*Rhamnus prinoidea*); *olkokola* (*Ximenia americana*); *oltimigomi* (*Pappea capensis*); *olasesiai* (*Osyris compressa*); and *olamuriak* (*Carissa edulis*).

After we finished the broth, the men took the goat meat down from the tree. From somewhere or nowhere, as soon as the soup was finished and the meat readied, the cooking site filled with people. Without a chopping block, Richard held up large hunks of boiled goat meat as the old man carefully, slowly, ritualistically, and with great concentration cut off small pieces. They both moved from person to person and then started over again, until everyone had as much as he wanted.

As with the Samburu and the Turkana, meat, milk, and blood are staples for nomadic Maasai. But even among the settled Maasai, the old traditions echo in their customs. For instance, when a young man wants to marry, his father approaches the bride-to-be's parents and opens the negotiations by saying, "I want your blood," meaning, "I want to unite our families." When a woman gives birth she is given blood soup, called *kirdi* in some areas and *sakalinja* in others. This soup given to new mothers is also shared by the rest of the family.

I was given the recipe for blood soup. A goat is freshly slaughtered, and 2 cups of fresh blood is taken from the neck artery. A rump steak is cut into small pieces. The fat of the stomach and the intestines is cut into pieces and is then melted in a large *sufuria*. The meat is added to the melted fat. A little water is added to the meat, which is fried until brown and until the fat begins to smoke, about 20 to 30 minutes. It is then cooled. The blood is strained, as it will clot if not absolutely fresh. It is then put into the warm meat mixture and stirred and cooked until the blood is brown.

Blood red plays a large part in the nomadic Maasais' dress. Against the backdrop of the dry plains, the Maasai nomads express themselves visually by plaiting red ochre into their hair and by dressing in brilliant red, pink, and orange togas and capes. The women adorn themselves in the same manner, but the emphasis is on blue and red. Although the women are shy, the men are not hesitant with their smiles, sound hospitality, and curiosity. I think they pity

179

me in my khaki trousers though, like a parcel done up in a plain brown paper wrapper that could have been gaily adorned.

Richard himself, his straw hat cocked jauntily on the back of his head, is every inch the modern Kenyan farmer-cum-businessman. Only the kitchen on Richard's land holds the last vestige of old traditions. It is the hut where his grandmother spent her last days. This round stick-and-mud house with its cone-shaped thatched roof has withstood enough dust, heat, and rain to grow tomatoes on its top. Inside, the earth has been packed hard by many feet over many years. The large cedar posts at the centre of the hut have been burnished a warm mahogany brown from the cooking fire that crackles now between the traditional three — but huge, oversize — rocks. This is a large cooking fire for a very large family, and like kitchens everywhere, it is the cosiest place on Richard's farm and the gathering place for family members. As I sit in this shelter, feeling quite at home sipping my afternoon tea, I have to pinch myself to believe that I am half a world away from my own roots. With warmth and high good humour, Richard has unreservedly welcomed me into the bosom of his remarkable family.

After a long day of cooking that started in the market at nine in the morning, after tramping through his forest with Aggrey sheke ole Mpario, and cooking soup, meat, and ghee out in the bush, Richard is still a bundle of energy and warm curiosity as we swap stories, search his dictionary, and discuss the merits of milk soured in a smoky gourd, a favourite drink all over Kenya. Then, just before dark, he walks me safely back to my door and, with a grin and a tip of his hat, disappears into the night

Maasai Preparation of Ghee

Ghee, similar to clarified butter, is prepared by boiling milk and scooping off the top cream. Each time milk is boiled during the day, the cream is removed and set aside until enough cream has been collected to make the ghee. The cooled cream, which is the consistency of soft butter, is then "washed" with water. That is, water is poured over the cream and any remaining milk leaches out and is poured off.

This cream is then boiled in a small sufuria over hot coals. As it boils, oil separates from the milk solids. This oil is then carefully poured off into a container. The remaining brown and crispy residue, which smells like a cake baking, is given to the children as a treat.

Ghee can be kept for as long as a year if a clean, dry spoon is used to remove it from its container for cooking purposes and the container is not left uncovered.

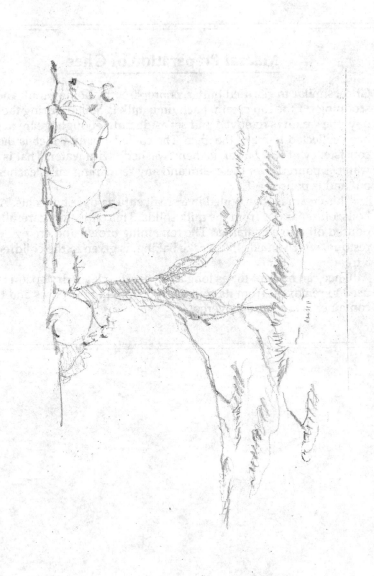

18
Robert Nicholas Mbalilwa

*I*n Nairobi, it's a rainy August morning and still winter on the equator. The African air outside Robert Mbalilwa's kitchen window is pungent with the smells of rain, maize, and the red Kenyan soil. Inside the kitchen, through the open window, the aura of earth and a silver, rain-laden sky mixes with the sweet smells of lemons and sugar as Robert prepares a Lemon Cream (page 190) for his employers, an English Court of Appeal judge and his Austrian wife. For the two of us, Robert has prepared African boiled tea — sweet, mild, and soothing — and we sip it as he prepares the dessert for a large dinner party that evening. In Kenya, cooking for ambassadors, judges, and politicians is a man's domain, and few are as gifted and as inventive as Robert.

A talented Luhya from Kenya's Western Province, Robert works and cooks in Nairobi, while his family remains in the hilly tribal land near the town of Kakamega, where he owns a small farm. Situated in a lush, rolling landscape, Robert's farm mostly grows beans and maize, but almost anything grows in Western Province. Cattle graze in the pasture lands, and water is plentiful.

Robert left farming seventeen years ago and left his wife to run the *shamba*. In Kisumu he took up cooking and was taught Austrian, French, and English cuisine. Although he readily and enthusiastically mastered the most foreign recipes imaginable, over time Robert slowly turned them into his own interpretations, to the delight of his employers, and over the years has added his own African touches. For his eclectic Afro-European dishes, Robert's small garden in Nairobi provides fresh fennel, basil, parsley, and rosemary — his favourites, which he adds to the plainest staples for the most amazing

results. For instance, he makes a vegetable dish of green pawpaws and fennel that has no equivalent among Western flavours, and he elevates cabbage above anything we have come to expect from this plain vegetable with a little tomato and a touch of basil, thyme, and oregano, his favourite combination of herbs.

Many of Robert's dishes are indecipherable to overtraumatized Western tastebuds. His careful blend of mild herbs is subtle. No single flavour stands out or overwhelms. If you are sick, tired, prone to tummy upsets, nervous, or stressed, Robert's cooking will miraculously heal and mend. He rarely serves anything raw, and he adds sugar and cream to his otherwise puckering salad dressing. Everything is calculated to soothe.

Although Robert is careful and meticulous in his philosophy, he is devil-may-care in practice. He gives hope to the most inept recipe follower. Robert's white sauce may look like paste and his wine sauce may be runny, but by the time they get to the table he has transformed the former into a lovely spinach soufflé and the latter into a creamy lobster sauce. He simply feels his way to perfection.

Today, Spinach Soufflé (page 187) starts off Robert's lunch. There are several kinds of leafy vegetables in Nairobi markets. One is *sukuma wiki*, which was brought into Kenya by Europeans as animal fodder. *Sukuma* is coarse, but it's not as bitter as spinach and is preferred by many Africans. Chopped fine and cooked with tomatoes and onions, it is delicious. *Mchicha* is another green, leafy vegetable with a small, tender leaf and a sweet taste. There is every kind of lettuce, and as for spinach, there are at least two kinds: One is a deep-green Italian spinach with broad leaves, and the other, home grown, is almost chartreuse in colour with a narrower leaf. When using the latter, Robert adds a pinch of bicarbonate of soda to turn the leaves the dark green that has come to be associated with soufflés.

Robert fiddles around with his spinach soufflé and adds one clove of garlic. Although a bit of nutmeg is standard, he puts in a generous pinch, and the combination gives Robert's soufflé a good deal of flavour. He doesn't sauce the soufflé, preferring to serve it dry, since he says it would shame him if it appeared on the plate standing in a puddle.

For the entrée, Robert is making short-crust cups filled with creamed mushrooms. The Short-Crust Cups (page 188) are the magic of this entrée. They should be a bit thick, not dainty, as this entrée is meant to be filling, like all good Kenyan dishes. The cups are a bit heavy by Western standards, but just carry on because the mushrooms are bathed in a feather-light sauce that compliments the buttery cups. The mushroom cups are served with sliced red-ripe tomatoes. Serve them, as well as the salad dressing, at room temperature. Again, this is an African cooking. Although taught by an Austrian, Robert has successfully repulsed all attempts at changing his basic attitudes and traditions. Just to get Robert to serve uncooked tomatoes is a feat. Everything he cooks is calculated to be easy on the stomach, and in his estimation, cold tomatoes in refrigerated dressing would clash with warm soufflé and warm, hearty mushroom cups. To make his point, he slips some sugar into the salad dressing. So Robert and Africa win in the end.

As for the Lemon Cream, don't serve too much of it, and choose very small glasses that have not been chilled. Again, this dessert is meant to be soothing, not sharp or cold. It's just too strenuous to follow a warm meal with a cold dessert and then with hot tea or coffee. These kinds of ups and downs are frowned upon and don't come naturally to Robert.

Lemons are grown at the coast, in the highlands near Mount Kenya, and in the gardens of Nairobi all year round. At this time of the year, the lemons in the markets resemble limes and the limes resemble lemons. Yet Robert has pulled the most perfect round, yellow lemon out of his hat. One thing about Robert: He's never at a loss. You would want him on a desert island; you would never starve. He can always be counted on to come sailing through any crisis, from no water and no gas to no electricity, with a smile still on his face. Recently he served a rolled sausage-stuffed roast that was only half cooked when the electricity went off and the oven died — yet he got it to the table on time and cooked to perfection. Robert is the kind of cook who can pat the bottom of a cast-iron pan and know whether or not he should add another egg yolk. Or he can cut 40 grams of butter to the nearest gram without weighing it.

In the kitchen, Robert is poetry in motion. He does everything with ease and with flair. He never gets worked up, and things that would defeat some cooks make Robert laugh. For all his nonchalance, he keeps a cool eye on everything that goes on in his kitchen, and when I'm finished with my tea, he pours me some more. Robert, laughing-light and warm-hearted, hides a shrewdness and a quickness to learn that makes him one of the best cooks in Kenya.

Spinach Soufflé

2 bunches spinach leaves, or 1 pound *mchicha* leaves
1 teaspoon salt
2 ounces butter (see Note)
2 ounces all-purpose flour (see Note)
1 cup milk
4 large garlic cloves, crushed
1/2 teaspoon ground nutmeg
1/2 teaspoon ground black pepper
4 large eggs, separated
1 chicken bouillon cube (optional)

Clean the spinach thoroughly, remove the stalks, and chop fine. Cover with water, add the salt, bring to a boil, and cook 5 to 6 minutes, or until the spinach is soft. Drain well and set aside. When cool, purée in the blender or press through a sieve.

Make a thick white sauce by melting the butter and adding the flour. Stir together over medium heat for a minute before adding the milk a little at a time, stirring constantly, until the mixture is thick and smooth.

Preheat the oven to 400°F.

Add the puréed spinach, garlic, and spices to the white sauce and mix well. Beat the egg yolks and mix in. If using the bouillon cube, crumble it into the mixture and blend thoroughly.

Beat the egg whites until stiff peaks form. Fold into the spinach mixture by carefully placing a metal spoon in the middle of the mixture, cutting to the bottom of the bowl, and bringing the mixture up and out to the sides of the bowl. Repeat until the egg whites are just blended in. *Do not* stir or overmix.

Pour the mixture into a greased 8-inch soufflé dish (a flat-bottomed, straight-sided ovenproof ceramic or glass bowl, not unlike a sufuria in shape). The bowl will be two-thirds full and the soufflé will rise as it cooks. Place in the middle of the hot oven. After 30 to 35 minutes, the top of the soufflé will be slightly golden brown. It is done when it springs back lightly to the touch. Serves 4

Note: For a denser soufflé, 3 ounces butter and 3 ounces flour is recommended.

Robert's Sweet and Creamy Dressing

2 tablespoons vegetable oil
1 tablespoon vinegar
2 tablespoons sour cream or light cream
1 tablespoon sugar
1/2 teaspoon salt
1/2 teaspoon dry mustard

Mix all ingredients together, blending well. Serve at room temperature. Makes about 1/3 cup

Short-Crust Cups

8 ounces all-purpose flour
Pinch salt
2 ounces margarine
2 ounces butter
3 tablespoons ice water

Sift together the flour and salt. Rub the margarine and butter lightly into the flour using your fingertips. Mix to a stiff paste with the ice water.

Form the cups by separating the mixture into 6 balls. Roll each between your palms to form thick "snakes" about 6 inches long. Coil each snake into a basket shape, smoothing out the surfaces.

Place on a baking sheet and cook in an oven preheated to 350°F. for 20 minutes. After 10 minutes, check the cups and prick the bottoms with a fork. The cups will be a very light brown when done. Cool well before filling with Creamy Mushroom Sauce with Oregano (recipe follows). Makes 6

Creamy Mushroom Sauce with Oregano

1/2 pound fresh mushrooms
1 ounce butter
1 tablespoon all-purpose flour
1 cup milk
1/2 chicken bouillon cube
Pinch dried oregano
Pinch ground black pepper
Pinch salt (optional)

Clean the mushrooms, remove the stems, and slice.
Make a cream sauce by melting and lightly browning the butter.
Add the flour and blend over low heat. Add the milk and simmer,
stirring, until the sauce begins to thicken. Add the 1/2 bouillon
cube, mushrooms, and oregano, and cook gently until the
mushrooms are tender but not overdone. Season to taste with
pepper and salt. The sauce should be light and slightly thin, but
not runny. Serves 6

Lemon Cream

3 eggs, separated
1/2 cup sugar
Juice and grated rind of 1 large lemon
1 cup whipping cream, beaten to form soft peaks

Mix well the egg yolks, sugar, lemon juice, and lemon rind. Cook,
stirring, over a double boiler until the sugar dissolves; or, if not
using a double boiler, cook very slowly over low heat. Remove
from the heat immediately and beat until the mixture changes from
yellow to white. Set aside and allow to cool completely.

Beat the whipping cream into soft peaks. Fold the lemon
mixture into the whipping cream. Beat the egg whites until they
form stiff peaks. Carefully fold the lemon-cream mixture into the
whipped egg whites and spoon into small serving glasses. If you
make this dessert well in advance, refrigerate it, but remove it from
the refrigerator at least 1 hour before serving. Serves 6

19

Tutti Hessel

*T*utti Hessel's house in Mweiga, not far from Nyeri, is a well-kept, much-loved memory of the English farmhouses first built in these parts by early European settlers. Her old, immaculate, vine-covered cottage is picturesquely perched on the edge of green rolling hills that dip into narrow valleys and up again, the green spreading out repeatedly over fertile, neatly cultivated farmland. Driving up the well-pruned, tree-lined drive to the house one is reminded of the early settlers' ability to transplant a little bit of England to the middle of Africa.

This highland area near the heavily forested Aberdare Mountains was originally the home of the Kikuyu tribe, and the struggle between black and white for this rich, fertile land became the focus of the Mau Mau rebellion, which in turn contributed to the move toward Kenya's independence. Known euphemistically among the settlers as "the Emergency," the rebellion emerged on the other side of the 1950s as full-blown Independence — formally declared in 1963. It was during these years of turmoil that Tutti began her life in Kenya as a new bride.

Her first home was a farm on the slopes of Mount Kenya overlooking the plains around Nanyuki. It was little more than a tent with an outdoor loo, which in turn was nothing more than a small clearing with a 360-degree view. She and her husband, Jens, bought the land with the help of an Englishman who had hired Jens as a farm manager and, five years later, felt that Jens deserved a farm of his own. Their first wheat crop paid off the owner of the local *duka*, who had given them seed on credit, and with their next crop they built a tiny, rough house with little to recommend it except that it was home.

Jens, a trained agriculturist, became so successful that Tutti soon unwillingly had to leave the tiny bridal house that they had built together on the mountain and move down onto the plains around Nanyuki to a proper house complete with English garden, rolling lawn, and beds of imported flowers that she only grudgingly came to love, missing the solitary challenge of her first home, where she had learned the independence of mind that characterizes her. In these early farm years she had preserved chilies and cucumbers, made her own cream cheese, and stored small tubs of homemade pork pâté in her kerosene fridge.

The best thing about moving down onto the plains was that Tutti had plenty of room for her vegetable garden. And her present garden, in Mweiga, as impressive as it is, has its inspiration in Tutti's days in Nanyuki. She has an extensive herb and spice garden with several kinds of chilies, coriander, caraway, dill, oregano, basil, rosemary, horseradish, several types of parsley, and chives, to mention just a few. Then there are vegetables such as potatoes, cucumbers, artichokes, curly kale, spinach, onions, lettuce, tomatoes, and, of course, maize. She grows a good number of fruits, including strawberries, mountain pawpaws, avocados, oranges, lemons, and limes. Just for good measure, or for good luck, in the centre of the vegetable garden is a thriving rose garden. Tutti's secret is that everything is fertilized with a rich mixture of grasses, leaves, twigs and the dung of several families of wild warthogs who have made Tutti's formal flower garden their refuge.

Tutti's first experience with animals began on her first farm on the slopes of Mount Kenya, which was at the end of a migratory route from the Aberdare Mountains, across the plains, and back again to Mount Kenya. It had always been Jens who shot game for the dinner table and who kept the farm free of foraging animals. Then, after Independence, when Tutti and her husband sold their farm in Nanyuki, he became a professional hunter, flying tourists-cum-hunters to remote corners of Kenya.

During these years, the gentle but tough farm cook became an even tougher game cook and tour caterer, roasting Thompson's gazelle and topi out in the bush, and catering safaris from the "market" that roamed through the camp. It was during this period that Tutti blossomed into a truly inventive cook, creating her own dishes and menu, often on the spur of the moment, for her pampered clients. While keeping her Danish pickled cucumbers and pork pâtés handy, she turned to an entirely new approach to cooking.

Tutti reckons that the best game meat in Kenya is Thomson's gazelle. She often uses the back ribs and prepares them simply. Skin the back and use the saddle between the shoulder blade and rump. Cut off the excess outer ribs to form the saddle. Thread smoked bacon between the ribs. The bacon is essential for moistness, as game meat is quite dry. Rub the meat with salt, pepper, and garlic. Place the saddle in a large roasting dish, if cooking in the oven, or in the centre of a large piece of aluminium foil if cooking over coals, and pour sour milk or yoghurt over the saddle. Steam, covered, for 2 hours; game meat always should be cooked until well done, never underdone. Remove the saddle from the pot or foil, and cut the ribs as in a prime-rib cut. Add flour to thicken the juices and 2 tablespoons red currant or cranberry jelly for an unforgettable gravy.

Tutti also has an especially beautiful way of preparing wild guinea fowl, pigeon, quail, or other small game birds: Twenty-four hours before cooking, you will need to set out 3 cups of cream, uncovered, to sour. When you are ready to cook, first rub the insides of the birds with rock salt, then stuff them half full with parsley and small dabs of butter. Add more parsley and more butter until each bird is well stuffed. Next, trim the fat from strips of bacon and wrap each bird with the fat and place in a heavy baking pan. (Tutti always uses a favourite enamel-lined iron pot, which cooks the dish evenly.) Skim off 8 tablespoons of the soured cream and drizzle over the tops of the birds. Add freshly ground black pepper. Sear the birds first in an oven heated to 425°F., then turn the oven to 350°F. and bake, covered, for about 1 1/2 hours.

Cooking on safari was not always easy for Tutti. The first time she tried to serve mock turtle casserole, she reached for a bottle of sherry, into which she found someone had poured Jay's Disinfectant. However, another disaster was turned to brilliant invention when a large silver tray full of pork chops, chicken pieces, and steak, made ready for the barbecue while her guests sipped their sundowners, was polished off by a four-footed bandit. Grimly fighting back tears, Tutti served all that she had on hand — potatoes and garlic — in a dish that has since become a staple in her kitchen. In a shallow baking pan layer 4 pounds diced cooked potatoes tossed in 1/2 pound melted butter laced with 20 crushed garlic cloves. Dot the top of the potato mixture with salt, pepper, more butter and garlic, and bake, uncovered, in a 400°F. oven for 20 minutes and serve with a fresh green salad.

Jens and Tutti no longer hunt for animals but take their clients on photographic safaris instead. And it was on one of these safaris that Tutti cooked a full Danish New Year's dinner in the bush by firelight. A practical romantic, her creation of a special night in Kenya reflects this philosophy. The New Year's Eve meal included a garlic-smothered goose stuffed with apples and prunes, served with pickled red cabbage, whole potatoes, and gravy made with the goose drippings and sweetened with red currant jelly. For dessert she served Danish Ris à l'Amande (page 198), a rice dish with a ritual similar to that surrounding English Christmas pudding. Instead of finding a coin in the dessert, the winning dinner guest must produce the only whole almond that has been placed in the pudding. Half an almond won't do, so everyone gums the pudding afraid of munching the prize almond and forgoing the table prize, a stash of homemade marzipan candies. Served with plenty of celebratory champagne, Ris à l'Amande provides a hilarious ending to the old year and a happy way to greet the new.

Even though the tough but romantic farm and safari years are mainly behind her, those days are still fresh in Tutti's mind and in her daily cooking. She still favours her farm menu of pâté, cheeses, and homemade brown bread for breakfast, and she still serves game birds for dinner. Always the Dane, still each day's cooking reflects Tutti's personal history — and nothing becomes her cooking more than her life in Kenya.

Tutti's New Year's Eve Dinner

New Year's Goose
Apple and Prune Stuffing
Boiled Potatoes
Red Currant Gravy
Sweet-Sour Red Cabbage
Ris à l'Amande with Cherry Sauce
Almond Confection

New Year's Goose

1 5 to 6-pound dressed goose
Coarse salt
2 tablespoons margarine (not butter or oil)
6 garlic cloves, crushed
Freshly ground black pepper
Apple and Prune Stuffing (recipe follows)

Rub the inside of the goose with a bit of coarse salt. Next, rub the goose all over with margarine, garlic, salt, and pepper.

Fill all the cavities, fore and aft, with the stuffing. Close the goose by securing the legs inside the tail flap. Place in aluminium foil with a small hole cut in the top for browning, or in a baking bag if you like. Place in an oven heated to 425°F. for 10 minutes. Then turn the heat to 350°F. and cook for approximately 2 1/2 hours, until the juices run clear when the thigh is pierced. During the last 10 or 15 minutes, remove the foil, or remove the goose from the bag, and either cook the bird to a crispy brown or grill briefly. Serves 6

Apple and Prune Stuffing

Peel, core, and cut into wedges 4 tart apples. Add 1 1/2 to 2 cups
pitted prunes. Mix the fruit together and sprinkle with white
pepper. Tutti never cooks this stuffing alone, only in the goose.
Makes enough for 1 6-pound goose

Red Currant Gravy

Skim off and reserve the fat from the drippings after the goose is
cooked. For each 1 cup of drippings, blend 2 tablespoons all-
purpose flour with 2 tablespoons water to make a thick, smooth
paste. Add the paste to the stock a little at a time, stirring
constantly over medium heat, until the gravy thickens. Add at least
1 heaping teaspoon of red currant or cranberry jelly to the gravy,
or more to taste. Do not add jam or soaked, sieved fruit. Makes 1
cup or more

Sweet-Sour Red Cabbage

1 red cabbage, finely sliced
1/4 cup salted water
1/2 cup vinegar
1/2 cup Ribena, or any blackcurrant concentrate (see Note)
1 tablespoon goose fat

Steam the cabbage in the water, vinegar, and juice until tender,
about 15 minutes in a pressure cooker, or 2 hours in a covered
saucepan. Uncover and add the goose fat. Serves 6

Note: If blackcurrant concentrate is unavailable, substitute 2 tablespoons
raspberry or red currant jelly and a squeeze of lemon.

Ris à l'Amande

2 1/2 ounces rice
2 cups milk
1 vanilla bean, cut in half, or 1/2 teaspoon vanilla extract
Pinch salt
2 ounces chopped, blanched almonds (see Note)
1 whole blanched almond
1 1/2 teaspoons almond extract
1 ounce sugar
4 teaspoons unflavoured gelatin
2 fluid ounces whipped cream, or 2 stiffly beaten egg whites

Simmer the rice, milk, vanilla bean (if using extract, reserve until later), and salt over low heat until the consistency is similar to a runny porridge or heavy soup and the rice is tender, about 15 to 20 minutes. Cool.

Combine the chopped almonds, whole almond (the prize), almond extract, and sugar and stir together. Gently add the almond mixture to the cooled rice and blend well.

Dissolve the gelatin in 1/8 cup water, add to the rice and almond mixture, and stir. (Add vanilla extract at this time, if using.) As the mixture settles and gels, carefully fold in the whipped cream or stiffly beaten egg whites. The consistency will be like a heavy soufflé. Pour into an 8-inch mould and chill for at least 3 hours. Serve with Cherry Sauce (recipe follows). Serves 6

Note: To blanch almonds, pour boiling water over them and let sit until the skins slip off easily.

Cherry Sauce

1 8-ounce jar or tin of cherries in their juice (do not use jam)
3/4 teaspoon corn flour (corn starch)
1 teaspoon almond extract

Spoon out 2 tablespoons juice from the cherries and set aside.
Bring the cherries to a boil in the remainder of the juice (add 1
tablespoon sugar if using sour cherries). Stir the corn flour into the
reserved juice. Blend together and add to the hot cherries.
Continue boiling until the mixture is clear and the consistency of a
white sauce, about 2 minutes. Add the almond extract and mix.
Pass with Ris à l'Amande pudding (page198). Makes about
1 1/2 cups

Almond Confection

2 tablespoons icing (confectioner's) sugar, sieved (see Note)
1 cup finely ground almonds
1 large egg white
1 teaspoon almond extract
Green food colouring (optional)
6 to 12 whole blanched almonds (see Note, page 198)
1/2 cup melted sweet or dark chocolate

Mix the sugar and ground almonds together. Add the egg white
and almond extract and use a palette knife to mix into a smooth
paste. (If you wish, add a little green food colouring to the
marzipan to give the candies a festive appearance.) Roll the paste
into a long, thin sausage. Cut into 1-inch pieces and roll into egg
shapes between your palms. Press 1 blanched almond into the
centre of each "egg," leaving the tip exposed. Holding the candies
by the almond, dip each halfway into the melted chocolate. Put on
wax paper or oiled paper to cool.   Makes 6 to 12

Note: The first 4 ingredients will be used to make marzipan. Substitute 1
250-gram package prepared marzipan if you wish and proceed with the
instructions.

Pili-Pili Sauce

Cover 1/2 pound small, hot red chili peppers with vodka and steep, covered, for 24 hours. Throw away the vodka, cover the peppers with good sherry, and let stand for 1 month. (Jens hotly debates the wisdom of throwing away the vodka). Put into a clean jar or a bottle with a shaker top and add to soups, eggs, or anything that can stand a bit of hot sauce.

Cream Cheese with Herbs and Spices

Pour 8 cups of whole milk into a large bowl, and leave standing at room temperature for 24 hours or even longer. Pour into a pan and bring nearly to a boil (the milk will curdle). Let cool slightly and pour into a bowl that has been lined with a slightly porous piece of cloth such as a nappy, muslin, or cheesecloth. Bring the cloth's edges together and secure with a rubber band. Hang the milk-filled cloth bag over the bowl and leave overnight to drain. Squeeze the bag several times until the liquid stops draining into the bowl.

In the meantime, prepare 1/2 cup of herbs and spices, including chopped chives, caraway seed, paprika or ground red pepper, crushed garlic, salt, and freshly ground pepper to taste.

Remove the cheese from the bag and empty into a fresh bowl. Stir in the herbs and spices and mix all together well. Roll into a small log if desired. Makes about 6 ounces

Cabbage Gâteau

2 pounds minced meat (preferably equal parts veal, pork, and beef)
1 large white onion, minced
Pinch salt
Pinch ground black pepper
3/4 teaspoon ground nutmeg
1/2 cup bread crumbs
2 large eggs, separated
3 medium cabbages
All-purpose flour
butter

Mix the meat and minced onion well. Add the salt, pepper, 1/2 teaspoon of the nutmeg, the bread crumbs, and the egg yolks and mix well. Beat the egg whites and fold in.

Parboil the whole cabbages in salted water for 3 to 5 minutes and carefully drain, reserving the liquid. Gently remove and separate the leaves. Grease well an ovenproof dish and line the bottom with the biggest cabbage leaves. Then add a 1-inch layer of cabbage leaves, followed by 1/2 inch of the meat mixture. (The cabbage leaves will reduce as they cook). Layer until all meat and leaves have been used, dusting each cabbage layer with flour. (Reserve a few of the large leaves to place over the last layer of cabbage leaves.) Dot the top with butter.

Cover and bake in an oven heated to 350°F. for 1 hour. Turn the gâteau out onto a warmed plate and slice.

Use the stock of the boiled cabbage and the juice of the gâteau for gravy. Bring the liquids to a simmer, remove a few tablespoons to a bowl, and stir in 1 tablespoon all-purpose flour for each cup of liquid. Stir this smooth paste into the hot liquid and add the remaining 1/4 teaspoon grated nutmeg. Continue simmering, stirring constantly, until thickened.

If there are leftovers, the gâteau is delicious sliced and served cold as a starter the next day. Or slice, brush with oil, and grill. Serves 8 to 10

Pork Pâté

3 ounces butter
3 ounces all-purpose flour
1 to 2 cups milk
1 pound pork liver
1 pound pork belly
1 50-gram tin anchovies, plus their oil (optional)
1 medium onion, puréed in a blender, or crushed with
a mortar and pestle
2 large eggs, separated
1 teaspoon salt
1 teaspoon ground black pepper
1/4 teaspoon ground ginger

Make a thick white sauce by melting the butter and adding the flour. Blend well together and add the milk a little at a time, stirring constantly, and simmer until thickened. Set aside.

Mince the pork liver and belly, together with the anchovies and their oil, putting the ingredients through the blender several times. Add the onion and heat the meat mixture in a large skillet until the fat in the pork melts. Add the egg yolks and stir well. Add 1 cup of the white sauce and the salt, pepper, and ginger. Stir and cool until lukewarm. Beat the egg whites until stiff peaks form and fold in.

Pour the pâté into small, well-greased tins or heatproof dishes. Arrange the uncovered tins or dishes in a shallow pan half filled with water. Bake for 60 minutes in an oven heated to 350°F. The pâté should be crispy brown on top. Cool. The baking dishes or tins can be put into the freezer after thoroughly cooling. Defrost overnight and serve for breakfast or at teatime with slices of wheat or rye bread. Makes about 2 1/2 pounds

Pickled Cucumbers

4 large fat cucumbers, approximately 2 pounds each
Salt
3 1/3 cups inexpensive white vinegar
4 cups good-quality white or brown vinegar
4 1/4 cups sugar
1 heaped teaspoon pickling spice

Peel the cucumbers, cut in half lengthwise, and remove the seeds. Rub with salt and let stand overnight in a bowl to drain. Throw away the brine and wipe the cucumbers dry.

Bring to a boil the inexpensive white vinegar and dip the cucumbers in it for 1 minute to make them crisp. Boil together the good-quality vinegar, sugar, and pickling spice. Boil until the sugar dissolves. With a fork, dip each piece of cucumber into the boiling sugar mixture for 1 minute. Put the cucumbers into a clean, sterilized jar.

Boil the sugar mixture 15 minutes longer. Skim frequently until clear. Pour over the cucumbers in the jar until covered. Seal as desired.

To serve, cut each cucumber half in strips. Use the cucumbers one at a time. Never put one back in the jar. If you have some cucumbers left over from a meal, put them in a small bowl with a little of the vinegar to keep them moist. Cover and refrigerate.

Light-as-a-Feather Birthday Surprise

1/2 ounce butter
1/2 cup bread crumbs
8 ounces ground almonds
6 1/2 ounces sugar
5 large egg whites, stiffly beaten
1 teaspoon almond extract
8 ounces dark chocolate, melted
1 overripe pineapple
1 1/2 pints whipping cream

Lightly grease 1 8-inch ring mould with the butter and dust with bread crumbs to prevent sticking. Mix the ground almonds with the sugar. Beat the egg whites until stiff peaks form. Fold in the almond mixture, then carefully fold in the almond extract. Spoon the mixture into the prepared mould. Bake in a moderate oven (300°F.) for 45 minutes, or until golden brown. Loosen sides and centre with a knife and gently turn the cake out onto a cooling rack.

Meanwhile, cut the pineapple into rings and each ring in half. When cool, coat the cake with the melted chocolate and leave to set. Place on a platter and arrange the halved pineapple rings around the base of the dessert to create a lace effect. Cube the remaining pineapple and use it to fill the centre. Whip the cream until stiff and serve separately. Serves 4 to 6

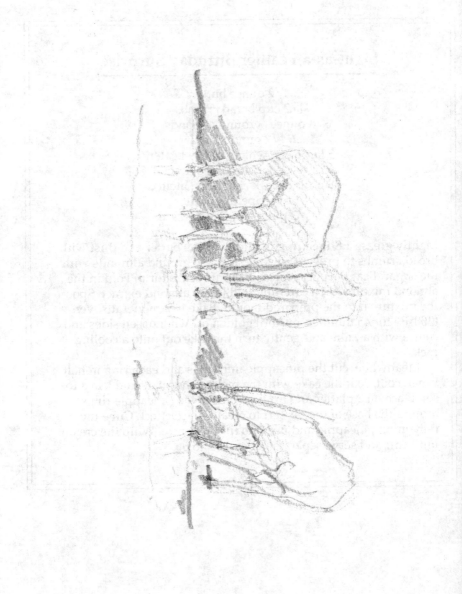

20
Waheeda Khan

W*aheeda* Khan's family history in Kenya is bound up in one of the most intriguing and dramatic events in modern Kenya history: the building of the Uganda Railway. Ambitiously begun in 1896 in order to secure the British presence in East Africa and operational by 1903, the railway was sometimes called the Lunatic Express. Originating in Mombasa and built over mountains, swamps, rain forests, rivers, the Great Rift Valley, and miles of brown scrub and rocky desert, the Uganda Railway ended not in Uganda but in Kisumu on the eastern edge of Lake Victoria. The railroad survives today as the main trading and commercial route through Kenya.

Waheeda's father came to Kenya from Afghanistan simply as Abdul Hamid Khan, one of thousands of coolies hired to work on the stretch of the railroad that was hacked out of the tsetse fly- and lion-infested desert between Mombasa and Nairobi. In Afghanistan, Abdul Khan always had been handy with a gun and never was known to waste two bullets when one would do the job. He could track game by smell and knew animal habits better than his own. So when he finally arrived in Kenya, he was given the job of advancing along newly laid track in a push trolley, covering the bush almost as a point man would for a small battalion in a guerilla war. And war it was: The elusive, brilliantly canny enemies of the men building the railroad were man-eating lions.

Man eaters are relatively rare, sweaty, dirty humans not being their usual cup of tea. A man eater is usually an old, wise, and clever adversary. One of the most amazing stories connected with the man eaters that Waheeda's father never tired of telling was the ordeal of

Charles H. Ryall. Ryall, who in June of 1900 had the bad luck to be the superintendent of Railway Police, was considered responsible for the apprehension of the man-eating lions of Tsavo. Abdul Khan was working on the railroad in Tsavo at the time, and in later years he spun out the tale for little wide-eyed Waheeda.

Since the lions scrupulously took only one man each night, Ryall thought he could easily outsmart the lone invaders with a small posse. What he found out the hard way was the depth of the lions' understanding of human nature and their shrewd ability to outsmart the superstitious workers and frustrated railroad managers. For instance, if a guard were mounted the lions would wait days, perhaps weeks, until the guard was relaxed. Then they would strike again, always taking only one man. Those nearby could hear the lions crunching the bones of the latest victim, and the panic spread until the men refused to work.

But Ryall thought he had a plan. He thought it an easy proposition. He would tether a goat to a Pullman car pulled out onto the lone track with nothing but plains as far as the eye could see on all sides. Then, with two men stationed at the Pullman windows within sight of the goat, he would wait. But tedium set in when two days went by and it looked as if the lion wouldn't show. The goat still bleated on its tether, the sun beat down on the blisteringly hot Pullman, and the cool nights lulled the men into dozing, just what the lion had been waiting for; besides, he preferred Ryall to the goat. After several days of tail-twitching patience, during one of Ryall's watches the old lion padded around the side of the Pullman farthest from the goat, quietly nosed open the door to the car, stalked down the aisle on its huge cat's feet, and, in one easy lightning flash, took Ryall with him out the window. That night the lion dined on the only armed guard in camp.

This is the story Abdul Khan told his daughter when she was very young. But when Waheeda grew older, others told her an equally amazing story about her own father.

It was while working as an advance man for the railway during the lion crisis that Abdul Khan spotted two immense male lions. They also had spotted him and had begun to advance upon him and the other four men on the push trolley.

Miles from help, Abdul quietly readied his rifle and ordered his four men up a nearby pole, which they wasted no time climbing, clinging to it for their lives. For Abdul had spotted not only the two males, but a small pride of females and cubs as well. Knowing that if

he shot the males, he'd be overwhelmed by several females, he decided to shoot the females first, hoping to divert the males' attention. In the din of gunfire, confusion, and slaughter, the two lions were indeed momentarily distracted. Abdul then took slow and careful aim and shot the first, heavily maned lion in the temple, the bullet passing through the man eater's head and killing the lion that accompanied him.

In the silence that followed, the four stunned workers who had witnessed the unbelievable spectacle of Abdul shooting two lions with one bullet clambered down the pole and began shouting, "*Simba Mbili, Simba Mbili* (He who shoots two lions with one bullet)," a name that stuck to Abdul Khan for the rest of his life.

Simba Mbili lived a long and eventful life and built a successful hunting lodge in the desert near the Tsavo River halfway between Mombasa and Nairobi and not far from the place where he shot the two lions. He had many European visitors, whom he took out into the bush hunting for weeks at a time. He had fame, fortune, and two wives, but Simba Mbili lacked one thing: children. Married twice to barren women, he prayed daily for at least one child. And when he was very old, he took a third wife, half Pakistani and half Kalenjin, who bore him Waheeda, meaning, in Arabic, "the only one."

Simba Mbili died in his seventies when Waheeda was only six. But in those six years he never let little Waheeda out of his sight and taught her to read and write his own language and to read and speak English, the only schooling Waheeda ever had. By the time he had Waheeda, Simba Mbili had had enough of killing, and he often took his little girl into the bush for weeks, teaching her the ways of the animals, spending nights in the trees, where Waheeda breathlessly watched the animals come and go at the water holes. She remembers the wheezing families of elephants stepping feather light, the shy gazelles and ponderous rhinos, the roars and snorts, trumpeting and snuffling in the night so full of life. Her father's love for her and his admiration for animals are Waheeda's fondest memories. It was of her father that she proudly spoke to me, and his stories are always on her mind.

Waheeda is a tall (5 feet 11 inches) woman who carries herself with quiet dignity. Long-necked and long-legged, her walk is reminiscent of those graceful animals she watched at the watering holes. Her movements as well as her speech are as unhurried as if she had all the time in the world, although she is a busy widowed mother of two strapping boys. But she takes the time to quietly curl up on the sofa, catlike, and tell me her story.

After her father's death, she lived with her mother and aunt until she was fifteen, when a marriage was arranged to a lusty, philosophical young man whom she had never met. With a small smile, Waheeda recalls her wedding. The days preceding an Asian wedding are marked by fireworks, singing, dancing, music, games, and, of course, eating. The day of the wedding itself is a prodigious feast. Asian meeting hall kitchens, where weddings are held, are huge and barn-like, sometimes 50 feet x 70 feet. Blazing wood fires are sunk deep in concrete trenches within the vast and cavernous space, upon which 2 x 3-foot vats are bubbling with sweet yellow rice, brilliant curries, and golden sweets. Lit only by slotlike windows running under the roof line, the shafts of hazy light that make it into the kitchen outline the darting bodies charged with stoking the fires and paddling the curries. Such kitchens would resemble nineteenth-century armouries, were it not for the sweet and pungent odours of cooking rather than the smell of molten metal.

Several rooms away from this beehive of activity, men and women eat separately. Throughout the day the bride remains separate from her new husband. In Waheeda's case, she was literally in the dark as to the identity of her husband until the bridal chamber door was shut behind her. Heavily veiled all day, it was her new husband, a complete stranger, who unveiled her when they were alone. At fifteen — shaking and timorous, desiring only her favourite doll — it was Waheeda's husband — six years her senior, understanding, and wise — who won her love and affection.

Waheeda proudly talks of her husband, who died suddenly eight years ago, and recounts a strange, mystical pattern of life when she tells me that he was an engineer with the railway, gone for weeks at a time on the route from Mombasa to Kisumu. It was during these long, lonely trips that he developed a love for the animals he watched roaming the plains. He would return to render these same animals in oils, watercolours, and pencil, drawing furious elephants with ears flapping and lions lazily enjoying family life. Her husband's pictures survive today as evidence of the blueprint pattern of Waheeda's life, a pattern that has given her a beautiful sense of composure and certainty. In her heart she carries the mysteries of nature as imparted by both her husband and her father.

But if there is an ethereal quality about Waheeda, it goes hand in glove with an elemental practicality born of the wisdom that has come from a hard life raising two boys on her own. Her outlook on life is anything but coy.

After her husband died, Waheeda turned to cooking to support her family. Now, working long hours in a restaurant, she still must begin her day by preparing lunch for her boys, who will warm up the food at noontime when she is at work. So in the early morning she cooks the biggest meal of the day before she even begins work at the restaurant. With a deadly sharp knife that disjoints and slices bone and without a chopping board, she neatly slices paper-thin onion rings into her palm and dices chilies between her fingers. Using a pressure cooker to save time, it is not surprising that simple dishes such as stews and boiled chops are her favourites. As for herself, after a day at the restaurant overseeing the preparation of samosas, cakes and fancy curries, Waheeda is content with meat and a little *ugali* and often too tired to eat more.

When she does have the time — usually on her day off — Waheeda cooks a blend of Asian and African food, a reflection of her roots and of Kenyan's modern history. For instance, she cooks us a mutton chop roasted in the pot, then steamed with green chilies, tomatoes and *sukuma wiki* and an up-country tomato-onion goat stew to which she adds fresh ginger, fresh garlic, turmeric, ground red pepper, and her own *garam masala*. She serves the stew with an easy, spicy raw onion salad and *chapati* which, like *ugali*, are used as knife, fork, and spoon. Then she finishes her spicy-hot meal with a mildly-sweet cassava dish that takes the fire right out of my mouth and brings me down to earth. Downright plain, it is nevertheless a soothing dessert and sticks in my memory as the perfect ending to a fiery meal.

The spiciest, hottest item in Waheeda's kitchen cabinet is a paste she makes of crushed garlic, ground red pepper, salt, and sugar. In mortar and pestle, crush 2 to 3 whole heads of garlic, or between 30 and 40 peeled garlic cloves. Then add as much ground red pepper as you wish. Waheeda's is the colour of ripe, red tomatoes, but wouldn't recommend going that far the first time around. Just pleasant brick red will do. Add a pinch of salt and a pinch of sugar. There is no end of possibilities for this paste, and it keeps for days without refrigeration. Put a dollop of the paste in mashed potatoes or stir a little into some softened cream cheese and spread thinly on toast. Serve the toast at teatime with sweet Somali Tea (page 54). Pass the paste around the table to spread on slices of roasted or boiled beef or marinate the beef first in a little oil mixed with the paste, then roast, grill, or fry the meat. Scramble it with your eggs. For a light lunch, the paste is nice in a white sauce to which you've added sliced hard-boiled eggs. Pour into pastry cups or over toast, and serve with a crunchy green salad. Or put a little paste in a white sauce and serve over pasta, tossing together well. Serve the pasta with thinly sliced steamed spinach. Waheeda eats her garlic–red pepper paste right out of the bowl with a spoon. "Clears the sinuses," she says, in a characteristic understatement.

To save precious time and energy, Waheeda is intensely organized. At her fingertips she keeps all she will need for almost everything she cooks. Her favourite spices are turmeric, ground red pepper, whole *jira* (cumin) seed, ground *jira*, *dhania* powder (ground coriander), salt, and her own homemade *garam masala*. She dips into these spices by the spoonful for almost every dish. Of her *garam masala* she says that it tastes like food, wrinkling her nose a bit at the thought of some *garam masalas*, which she describes as too much like perfume.

Another example of the way Waheeda has ordered her life is her pantry or store. It is the picture of organization. All her spices are home ground and neatly stored in tightly closed jars. *Garam masala*, properly stored, will last at least two years. Waheeda's is a small pantry, space- and time-saving, efficient, and ordered for easy access as well as holding the sum total of all her needs. Everything has its place. There is absolutely nothing haphazard about Waheeda.

Although her life is simple due to her long working hours, and even though her home duties take up any leisure time, Waheeda's door is always open to friends, relations, and neighbours. Spring blooms inside her house and out, as vines cover the walls of her hallway as well as frame her doorway. On one of her days off, Waheeda and I sit outside in the light morning air as she dries her long, black hair which is covered with a goo of henna. Lunch simmers in her kitchen as we await the arrival of her sons, neither of whom works on the railroad or is interested in wild animals. For once she talks about herself and her dream of visiting her father's homeland, a land of beautiful flowers, open spaces, animals, mountains, lakes, and streams: the lasting vision cut from her childhood days when she lived the things she dreams.

Chicken *Tikka*

1 1/2 tablespoons crushed fresh ginger
1 1/2 tablespoons crushed fresh garlic
4 green chili peppers, chopped
2 tablespoons chopped fresh *dhania*
Juice of 2 large lemons
1 tablespoon vinegar
1 teaspoon salt
Pinch ground red (cayenne) pepper
1/4 teaspoon ground turmeric
1 teaspoon *garam masala* (page 220)
3 tablespoons plain yoghurt
4 tablespoons vegetable oil
1 3-pound chicken, quartered and skin scored so that
it will absorb the spices

Grind together the ginger, garlic, chilies, and *dhania* with a mortar and pestle. Add the lemon juice, all the other spices, yoghurt, and oil. Toss with the chicken pieces and marinate at room temperature for 3 hours.

Put on the barbecue over hot coals, turning often and brushing with oil until the chicken is well browned and cooked through.
Serves 4

Spicy Goat Stew

1 large onion, chopped
3 tablespoons vegetable oil
1 teaspoon crushed garlic
1 teaspoon crushed fresh ginger
3 large tomatoes, chopped
1 teaspoon ground red (cayenne) pepper
1 teaspoon *garam masala* (page 220)
1 teaspoon salt
1 2-pound goat (or lamb) leg, cut by the butcher into bite-size
pieces, including the bone
3 cups water
2 medium potatoes, peeled and cubed
1/2 cup coarsely chopped french green beans
1 tablespoon finely chopped fresh *dhania*

Fry the onion in the oil until crisp. Add the garlic, ginger, and tomatoes and cook until all is a thick paste. Add the spices, salt, meat, and water. Cover and cook until the meat is tender. If necessary, add a little more water, then add the potatoes and green beans and cook until tender. Uncover and cook until the sauce is very thick. Before serving, stir in the *dhania*. Serves 4

Boiled Mutton Ribs with *Sukuma Wiki* and Chilies

1 medium onion, chopped
3 tablespoons butter or margarine
3 medium tomatoes, coarsely chopped
4 green chili peppers, finely chopped
1 teaspoon salt
1 2-pound mutton rib section, cut into chops
3 cups chopped *sukuma wiki*, cabbage, or spinach

In a large pot, fry the onions in the butter or margarine until translucent. Add the chopped tomatoes, chilies, and salt and cook together until well blended and a bit soft. Add the ribs, cover with water, and simmer 25 minutes. Add the *sukuma wiki* or other vegetable and 1/2 cup water. Cover and simmer again 20 minutes (10 minutes if using cabbage or spinach). Uncover and cook until the water evaporates. (Cabbage should be a bit underdone.) There will be no sauce with this dish. Serve with *ugali*, rice, or *chapati*. Serves 4

Chapati

3/4 cup water (approximately)
4 1/2 cups fine-ground whole-wheat flour (Atta; see Note)

Add the water to the flour a little at a time until the dough is pliable. Knead deeply with the knuckles for several minutes. Nip off golfball-size chunks of dough and roll into neat balls. Press the balls a bit flat between your palms and dip both sides into a pan of flour, thoroughly coating the dough. Roll out to about 6 inches in diameter; avoid overrolling the dough. Place on a medium-hot, dry, shallow or flat iron pan. Cook briefly on each side, turning once. Turn again and press down on the *chapati* with your fingers or a spatula while rotating it on the pan. The dough will bubble a bit. Remove to a plate before it gets too brown, and keep warm in the oven, covered, until all are cooked. Serve hot. Makes about 16

Note: If Atta is not available, use a mixture of 2/3 whole-wheat flour and 1/3 all-purpose flour.

Whole Fish *Masala*

1 or 2 whole tilapia, or 2 pounds fillets
Juice of 1 lemon
1/4 teaspoon salt
1 medium onion, chopped
1 teaspoon ground cumin
3/4 cup vegetable oil
2 medium tomatoes, chopped
1 teaspoon crushed garlic
1 teaspoon crushed fresh ginger
2 green chili peppers, finely chopped
1/2 teaspoon ground red (cayenne) pepper
1/2 teaspoon *garam masala* (page 220)
Pinch salt
2 tablespoons chopped fresh *dhania*

Do not skin the fish, but cut it into large pieces with a sharp knife, slicing directly through the fish widthwise, removing the tail but saving the head.

Combine the lemon juice and salt and place the fish in this marinade for at least 1 hour.

In a large skillet, fry the onions and cumin in 1/4 cup of the oil until brown. Add the tomatoes, garlic, ginger, chilies, ground red pepper, *garam masala*, and salt. Simmer over medium-high heat until the sauce is thick.

Drain the marinade from the fish. Fry the fish in the remaining 1/2 cup oil until brown. Put the fish directly into the sauce, and simmer on low heat for 10 minutes.

Add the *dhania*. Remove from the heat, cover, and let stand for 10 minutes. Serve with *ugali, chapati,* or rice. Serves 4

Rashmi Kebab

1 chicken breast
1 green chili pepper, chopped
1 tablespoon chopped fresh *dhania*
1 teaspoon crushed fresh ginger
1 teaspoon crushed garlic
Pinch ground turmeric
1/4 teaspoon ground red (cayenne) pepper (optional)
1/2 teaspoon *garam masala* (page 220)
Pinch salt
Juice of 1/2 lemon
2 tablespoons vegetable oil
2 bamboo or metal skewers

Remove the breast meat from the bone and cut into about 12 cubes
for threading on barbecue skewers. Pulverize the chilies, *dhania*,
ginger, garlic, spices, and salt in a blender or liquidizer, or grind to
a paste with a pestle and mortar.

Squeeze the lemon juice over the cubed chicken. Mix the paste
with the oil and spread over the meat, mixing it in well. Marinate
at room temperature for at least 1 hour.

Thread the chicken onto the skewers and barbecue over slow
coals for 15 to 20 minutes, turning as necessary. Remove the
chicken from the skewers, and serve with rice and a salad of sliced
carrots, onions, and green peppers. Serves 1

Garam Masala

1/4 teaspoon coriander seed
1/4 teaspoon whole cloves
2 cinnamon sticks
1 tablespoon *jira* (cumin) seed
1 teaspoon whole black peppercorns
1/4 teaspoon husked cardamom seed

First, coarsely grind all the ingredients with a mortar and pestle as the mixture will be too rough for a conventional blender. Then grind all together in the blender to form a fine powder. Store in a glass jar with a tight-fitting lid. Do not store in a plastic container, as the oils that give the spices their flavour will evaporate.
Makes about 1/4 cup

Onion Salad

2 medium purple onions, thinly sliced
Juice of 1/2 lemon
1/2 teaspoon ground red (cayenne) pepper
1/2 teaspoon salt
1 teaspoon sugar
4 medium tomatoes, grated (see page 73) or skinned and chopped

Put all the ingredients into a bowl and toss until the onions are well coated. Serve with any dish, accompanied by rice or *chapati*. This is especially good with Special Fried Rice (page 141). Serves 4

Sweet Cassava Pudding

1 pound cassava, peeled and cut into small bite-size chunks
2 cups milk
1/2 cup sugar
4 cardamom pods, husked and seeds crushed
Raisins
Crushed almonds

Cover the cassava with water and bring to a boil. Simmer until the cassava is still a little firm, about 15 to 20 minutes. Remove from the heat and drain.

In another saucepan, heat the milk, sugar, and cardamom, and cook gently just until the sugar melts. Add the cassava to the milk and simmer until the sauce has thickened and the cassava pieces are soft but not mushy. Cool and refrigerate. Spoon into bowls and decorate with raisins and crushed almonds before serving.
Serves 2 to 4

Rice Pudding

1/2 cup rice, soaked overnight in water to cover
2 cups milk
1/4 cup sugar
4 cardamon pods, husked and seeds coarsely ground,
or 1/4 teaspoon ground cardamom
1 tablespoon chopped almonds
1 tablespoon raisins or sultanas

Drain the soaked rice, wash, and place in a saucepan. Cover with 2 inches fresh water, bring to a boil, and cook until the water evaporates, approximately 15 minutes. Add the milk to the hot rice and stir well. Bring to a boil again. Add the sugar, cardamom, almonds, and raisins or sultanas. Mix well and simmer until the pudding is just thickened. This is delicious served hot in the morning as a cereal or served cold in the evening as a pudding.
Serves 2 to 4

Glossary

All-purpose flour:	plain flour.
Ayah:	nursemaid.
Bay leaf:	laurel leaf.
Bell pepper:	sweet pepper, capsicum.
Bhajia:	savoury fried vegetarian snack.
Chakula:	food.
Chapati:	round, flat unleavened bread cooked on a griddle.
Chili:	chile or chilli; a hot pepper, red or green.

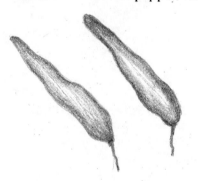

Cooker:	stove.
Corn starch:	a very fine corn or maize flour.
Cumin:	*jira*.
Curry:	a spicy, thin sauce.
Curry leaves:	curry leaves.

| *Debe:* | 5-gallon or 20-litre tin or plastic containers; originally they hold paraffin or cooking oil and are recycled for use in transporting water, charcoal, and other goods. |

Dhania:	herb also known as fresh coriander or cilantro.
Dhania jira:	powdered spice mixture that includes equal parts ground coriander seed and ground cumin seed.
Dhow:	single-masted sailing vessel flying a tricornered sail whose design is of great antiquity.

| *Duka:* | small shop. |

| *Garam masala:* | spice mixture used to flavour meat dishes; see page 220 for recipe. |
| Ghee: | cooking fat extracted from cream. |

Hoteli:	restaurant or informal café.
Icing sugar:	confectioner's sugar.
Jiko:	small one-burner stove or cooker that uses either charcoal or kerosene.
Jira:	cumin; sometimes spelled *jeera*.
Jua kali:	"do-it-yourself" products and projects.
Kanga:	long, decorative cloth worn around the waist.
Kifumbu:	a cone-shaped, basket-woven implement used to "milk" coconuts.

Lodge:	tourist hotel.
Maize:	corn.
Maize or corn flour:	cornstarch.
Maize meal:	cornmeal.
Mandaazi:	deep-fried sweets similar to doughnuts.
Masala:	a spicy, thick sauce.
Matatu:	taxi-bus that is the main form of public transportation in Kenya.
Matoke:	a hard, lightly lemon-flavoured banana with the texture of a potato that is used mashed in a dish that is also called *matoke*. Unripened dessert bananas can be substituted when *matoke* bananas are not available.
Mchicha:	ground-crawling, small-leafed vegetable similar to spinach in taste and texture.
Minced beef:	ground beef.
Morani:	warriors.

Mzee: old one; used as a term of respect.

Nyama: meat.

Omena: small dried fish.

Pawpaw: papaya.
Pilau: rice cooked with various spices.
Pili-pili
  (or *piri-piri*): spicy hot; also, ground hot red peppers.
Posho: maize meal *ugali*.

Self-raising flour: self-rising flour.
Sesame seed: sim sim.
Shamba: small vegetable garden or farm.

Shuka: piece of cloth worn tied around the waist by men.
Sim sim: sesame seed.
Sour cream: cultured cream.
Sugar: caster, white, or granulated sugar (*not* icing or confectioner's sugar).

Sukuma wiki:	"stretch the week"; a popular, coarse green leafy plant similar to collard greens that is the foundation of many meals.
Sufuria:	a round, lightweight aluminium cooking pot without handles that comes in sizes ranging from very small to more than 2 feet in diameter.
Thick coconut milk:	see pages 69–70 and 90 for explanation and instructions.
Thin coconut milk:	see page 69–70 and 90 for explanation and how-to.
Ugali:	a semihard cake made of maize or millet meal that usually accompanies meat stews and *sukuma wiki*.
Uji:	porridge made from millet flour or a commercially packaged mixture of millet flour, maize meal, and powdered milk.

Author Index

Recipe Index